MY LIFE HIS MISSION

TRUE STORIES
FROM STUDENTS
LIVING ON THE EDGE

KIM P. DAVIS

INTEGRITY®
PUBLISHERS
family

Nashville

MY LIFE, HIS MISSION

Published by Integrity Publishers, a division of Integrity Media, Inc., 660 Bakers Bridge Ave., Franklin, TN 37067

HELPING PEOPLE WORLDWIDE EXPERIENCE *THE* MANIFEST PRESENCE OF GOD.

Cover Design: Roy Roper, Wideyedesign
Interior Design: Kimberly Sagmiller, Visibility Creative

Library of Congress Cataloging-in-Publication Data [to come]
ISBN 13: 978-1-59145-488-5
ISBN 10: 1-59145-488-3

Printed in the United States of America
06 07 08 09 LBM 9 8 7 6 5 4 3 2 1

CONTENTS

CONTENTS

ACKNOWLEDGMENTS

I am amazed and grateful to our loving Father, who is behind the Voices of the Faithful books. Beth Moore and I stood in awe as we watched what God was doing on the devotional. I never would have dreamed that a student book would come next.

To the students who contributed stories of their mission trips, I thank you. You are living on the edge for God, and He is watching you with enjoyment! Thanks also to the students and leaders who participated in pilot groups and others who made contributions.

This book could have not been written without the assistance of many friends at the International Mission Board. Thank you, Mike, Felicity, Kelly, Dan, Tracy, Van, Ricky, Craig, Wendy, Terri, Clyde, Les, Chip, Pam, Tonya, Amy, Chuck, and Sheryl.

Without Jeremy Welborn's writing suggestions for a student audience, I would not have been able to complete this book. Thank you, Jeremy.

To the good people at Integrity Publishers, you have been great to work with again. You believed in the Voices of the Faithful books from the beginning. Jennifer Stair, thank you for editing.

To my faithful prayer warriors who prayed while I wrote, thanks for taking on this second project. God answered your prayers.

And finally, I want to thank my husband, D. Ray, who was my sounding board. My son Paul let me know when I needed to rephrase something in a lesson. Emily and Trevor, thanks for the extra chores you did around the house so that I could write. I also want to thank my parents and in-laws for their support. I love you all very much.

IMPACT THE WORLD ON YOUR KNEES

Have you ever asked, "Can I really make a difference for Christ?" The answer is yes! Through prayer, you can change the world. There are many things we can *do*, such as use our talents and abilities to accomplish some great work for the Lord. However, *being* in communion daily with the Father and remembering in prayer the work that is advancing His kingdom on earth are extremely important.

James O. Fraser was 22 when he became a pioneer missionary to the Lisu people group in China. After many struggles in starting the work, he wrote in a letter to a friend, "I am feeling more and more that it is ... the prayers of God's people that call down blessing upon the work, whether they are directly engaged in it or not. ... Christians at home can do as much for foreign missions as those actually on the field. I believe it will only be known on the Last Day how much has been accomplished ... by the prayers of earnest believers. ... Solid, lasting missionary work is done on our knees."[1]

God says, "Ask of me, and I will make the nations your inheritance, the ends of the earth your possession" (Ps. 2:8). God is willing for the gospel to be taken around the world. All you have to do is ask!

There are many ways you can pray for God to bring the gospel to the nations. Start by praying for the millions of people all over the world who do not know Christ. Check to see if your church has adopted a specific people group—people who have a unique culture and language. If your church hasn't yet chosen a people group, go to www.imb.org and click "people groups" to choose a people group to pray for.

When you decide to make a difference in the world by praying regularly for a specific people group, here are some things you can pray for:

1. Pray that God will glorify Himself through His work among this people group.

2. Pray for unity, boldness, and encouragement among believers in the country.

3. Pray for churches in the country to reach out to meet the needs of the people.

4. Pray that God would protect Christians in the country as they share the gospel.

5. Pray for the Lord to send missionaries to this people group.

6. Pray that people will become open to hearing about Jesus and will become believers.

7. Pray for the salvation and witness of those in positions of leadership in the country.

Many Christian missions organizations have Web sites that provide prayer requests for their missionaries and people groups. For instance, the International Mission Board (IMB) Student Mobilization Team (www.thetask.org) has regional links that connect you to specific prayer requests for people in different regions of the world. A daily devotional called *Voices of the Faithful*, written by Beth Moore and hundreds of missionaries, gives you a daily opportunity to pray for specific requests concerning what God is doing in the world (www.voicesofthefaithful.com).

Perhaps the best way for you to get a passion to pray for the people of the world is to go on a mission trip. When you are confronted with firsthand evidence that people have not heard of Jesus or believed in Him, you will understand how much we need to pray.

When teaching His disciples how to pray in Matthew 6:9–13, Jesus asked His Father, "Thy kingdom come, Thy will be done, on earth as it is in heaven" (NASB). The verb for "will be done" means "to be fulfilled, to bring to pass, to be finished."

What is God's will that He wants to be accomplished? "That the world should be saved through Him" (John 3:17, NASB). God wants every nation to believe and turn to Jesus. Second Peter 3:9 says, "The Lord is not slow about His promise, as some count slowness, but is patient toward you, not wishing for any to perish but for all to come to repentance" (NASB).

All believers—including high school and college students!—can pray in God's will for people groups across the world to hear the gospel and to become Christians. So choose to make a difference in the world ... PRAY!

YOUR PRAYERS CAN CHANGE THE WORLD

What if every Christian student on your campus or in your church began to pray that every people group would hear the gospel? Could your prayers really affect the world?

In Matthew 9:36–38, Jesus reveals that prayer is the first step to evangelism. "When he saw the crowds, he had compassion on them, because they were harassed and helpless, like sheep without a shepherd. Then he said to his disciples, 'The harvest is plentiful but the workers are few. Ask the Lord of the harvest, therefore, to send out workers into his harvest field.'"

Notice that Jesus did not say, "Get out there and win some souls!" Instead, with a heart filled with compassion for the lost, He told His disciples to pray, asking the Father to send out workers.

We know that God is patiently waiting for the world to repent (2 Peter 3:9), but He is also patiently waiting for His followers to share the good news throughout the world. We are a part of that plan every time we pray for God to send workers to take the gospel to the nations.

As we pray that God will compel believers to take His message to the world, we are bringing the return of Christ closer. "And the gospel of the kingdom shall be preached in the whole world for a witness to all the nations, and then, the end shall come" (Matt. 24:14, NASB).

Wesley Duewel, who served as a missionary to India for more than 25 years, writes, "Your prayer for world harvest can be more effective today because God in His sovereignty is coordinating world trends to make rapid fruitfulness available to His children. If we will put priority on prayer and obedience, this can be earth's greatest harvest time. ... There is no limit to what any Christian can accomplish through prayer!"[2]

Praying for the world will not only make a positive difference in people around the world coming to Christ, but it also will change you.

Your focus on the gospel will extend to the great, big world God wants to redeem. If you are praying for a specific people group, you are going to be interested in that people group. Before you know it, you'll want to find out more about the people: their customs, their language, and their ideas about religion. You will be drawn to them, and eventually, you may visit their land on a mission trip.

A boy began praying for a people group in Albania over 15 years ago. He prayed daily for them, and his family began praying with him. As a result of their prayers, the boy and his father took a mission trip to this atheist country. God worked in their hearts through their prayers and the mission trip, and his family moved to Albania as missionaries. The father, who was a lawyer, was able to help write the new constitution for the government that allowed freedom of religion after years of spiritual darkness. The prayers of just one teenager helped to open the door of this nation to the gospel!

Meryl from Anderson College also prepared herself for a mission trip through prayer.

> A secretary on campus asked me to consider going to South Asia on her daughter's team. I prayed He would put me in places of utter dependence on Him. He did. I traveled to the other side of the world, trekked up to 12,450 feet altitude, and taught students who did not really understand me, in hopes that I could tell them about Jesus. Only one individual in the area was a follower of Christ. The rest were Buddhist. The Lord miraculously brought people into our paths with whom we got to share His story.
>
> The Father showed me that summer that *all* is for His glory, and life does not work without prayer. He is in control, and He

*simply lets us participate in His work by His grace. ... My team did not see any of our new friends come to Jesus, but He allowed us to plant seeds, give Bibles, and cover that place with prayer. After we left, **He** saved 13 people in that village through workers who continued to share His good news.*

Prayer will prepare you to make a difference in the world, just like it did for Meryl. When you pray for God to send out workers, He will provide opportunities for the gospel to be shared. Even if you never go on a mission trip, you can touch the world through prayer. And you will be forever changed.

APPLY IT

1. In Matthew 9:36–38, what did Jesus ask His disciples to do? How can you specifically be involved?

2. Read Isaiah 65:24. Who do you think initiates prayer: God or man? Explain.

3. Read Hebrews 7:25. How can Jesus' example of praying for others affect our own prayers?

For further study (optional):
From what you've learned in this lesson, write a prayer to the Father.

EVERYONE CAN PRAY

We learned yesterday that prayer is the first step to evangelism. Through prayer, every Christian can participate in the Great Commission to make disciples of all nations (Matt. 28:19–20). Not everyone can go on a mission trip, but every believer can pray.

Perhaps you are excited about changing the world by praying for the nations, but like many students, you may be wondering, "How do I start?" In Matthew 6:9–13, Jesus gives us a great example of how to pray: "Our Father in heaven, hallowed be your name, your kingdom come, your will be done on earth as it is in heaven. Give us today our daily bread. Forgive us our debts, as we also have forgiven our debtors. And lead us not into temptation, but deliver us from the evil one."

In this prayer, Jesus' first concern is that God is glorified in all the earth. Then He praises the Father and asks that His will be done. Next, Jesus reveals that we should ask the Father to meet our daily needs, then He instructs us to ask for forgiveness and to forgive others. Finally, we are to pray to be delivered from Satan and temptation.

If you are interested in changing the world through prayer, then follow Jesus' example by asking God to glorify Himself through you. Pray for God to send out workers to take the blessing of salvation through Christ to all peoples. Ask Him to meet any spiritual, physical, or financial needs that missionaries around the world may have. Confess sin such as unbelief and pride, and forgive others who may persecute you or other students who are considering being missionaries. When Satan throws doubts and difficulties your way as a result of praying for the nations or saying yes to a mission trip, ask God to help you resist the enemy and the temptation to doubt God's sovereignty and faithfulness.

As you pray, God's presence will be with you, perhaps like never before. Through prayer, you are allowing yourself to be totally dependent on Him. Scripture tells us that God is near to those who pray: "Draw near to God and He will draw near to you" (James 4:8, NASB).

Kristina from Midwestern State University said,

Prayer is so unique and important. It is a time where we can come before our God and communicate, not with mere speech or expression, but with our deep inner soul and heart. It gives birth to a whole new depth to the relationship we have with our holy Lord. How amazing this is! We can connect with the God of the universe.

Visiting a Muslim cemetery in Central Asia, it felt as if I were stepping around the bodies of those lost in a battle. I felt so saddened for my Lord, because His heart must ache deeply for people who die without Him. I decided that I will not stand by and watch people live and die without the knowledge of Jesus Christ. So what now? I must pray. How do I know where to go, what to do, or how to do it without first asking God? Prayer is vital to know His will. And when it comes to prayer, I have never known God to be anything but faithful and true.

If you know students going on a mission trip, offer to be part of their prayer team. They will be blessed by your prayers, and you will be blessed by praying for them. If you're not sure where to start, two great Web sites that provide information and requests for global prayer are www. imb.org/compassionnet and www.thetask.org/students/G_ Passion/prayer.htm.

If you are considering being a student missionary, you need to fall on your knees right now and begin praying for God to make His plans clear to you and to prepare you for your trip.

Hunter, a high school student from North Carolina, was serious about prayer in preparation for her mission trip.

> After accepting the call to go to Swaziland, I needed to find a prayer partner. My grandmother had just died, and I asked the person who had been the most supportive of me during that time. We would routinely pray together either at school or on the telephone. We prayed for safe travel for the mission team, safety for my mother and my brother who would remain at home while my dad, sister, and I traveled, and that God would use me to share His love.
>
> He continued to pray for me while I was overseas, along with a large group of people from my family and church. The evidence of their prayers was seen daily in Africa. Because we were guided by God and open to His direction, we were able to lead people to Christ.
>
> The prayers continued when I returned home. Adjusting back to life at home was not easy, but again I was able to do so through prayer. This trip taught me about God's faithfulness to His children and how He provides for those who are called according to His purpose.

Don't miss out on the incredible opportunity to pray for the nations and for those whom God calls to take the gospel to the world. As O. Hallesby says, "Prayer is the most important work in the kingdom of God."[3]

APPLY IT

1. Commit to pray regularly for world missions, and make a list of people you would like to ask to pray with you.

2. Reread from this week's introduction the specific requests for the people group you are praying for. Make your own prayer strategy, using these requests and adding other requests.

3. Write a personal prayer that is patterned after the Lord's Prayer.

For further study (optional):
Jesus intercedes in prayer for you. Read John 17:6—26 and list exactly how He prays for you. You will be blessed by reading this passage!

PRAYERWALKING FOR PEOPLE GROUPS

Jesus walked a lot. As He walked, He saw many people who were harassed and helpless (Matt. 9:36). It's not hard to imagine that as Jesus walked and saw the people, He prayed to His Father concerning people who needed Him. The Savior likely prayed on-site for people and asked God to send out workers to reach them.

That's what prayerwalking is. It's praying purposely and on-site for specific people. And it often involves walking. The term "prayerwalking" is not a word from the Bible, but walking is mentioned in the spiritual sense of intimate relationship with the Lord. Enoch and Noah both "walked with God" (Gen. 5:21–24; 6:7–9). Everything they did reflected a relationship with the Creator.

Our physical walking can reflect our friendship with God as well. As we walk, we can pray for the people we pass on the street or in the buildings we walk by, praying specifically for salvation or for some other request. In 1 Thessalonians 5:17, we are encouraged to "pray continually." Praying as we walk is just one more way to participate in this command. We shouldn't pray to draw attention to ourselves, but we should pray quietly to draw our attention and God's attention to specific people.

You can prayerwalk locally or internationally when praying for specific people groups. Perhaps, for example, you feel led to pray for people groups from India. Most people from India who are living outside their homeland have a cultural center where they meet. If there is one in your community, you can go to this site and pray for the people on the public space in front of the building.

Many students go on a mission trip for the purpose of praying on-site for a people group. Cortney from Florida State University was led to be involved in a prayerwalking project in a rural Muslim village overseas.

My partner and I were instructed to prayerwalk an entire district in one month. We experienced God in ways I never knew I could experience Him. I watched Him break down strongholds as we prayed over mosques and temples, and I felt the presence of evil like I never had before.

One day we saw a new housing development. It had been a long, hot day, but the Spirit was nudging us forward. We tried to convince Him that it was better for tomorrow. But He would have no excuses. So we stood in front of 102 houses and spoke the name of Jesus into each one—claiming this house, this ground for the glory of Jesus Christ long before anyone was able to claim it in the name of Allah, Buddha, or Vishnu. And God did some preemptive work in that land, which is claimed in the name of the one, true God who will reign victoriously forever.

Ryan from Mississippi College and his teammate prayed for a specific people group on-site as they looked down on villages from the Himalayas.

As I stood on top of a mountain, it all became clear to me. **Yes, Father, I will,** I prayed as I looked at nine villages in three directions and uttered a prayer that the gospel of Jesus Christ would be brought to these people. . . .

On the pinnacle, I could see for 20 miles in one direction, 10 in another, and 15 in another. There were villages almost literally beneath my feet, and some that would take days to reach. Each is almost totally full of lost people. I came down from the mountain and out of the Himalayas knowing that I fulfilled my purpose.

Jamie from Oklahoma Baptist University went on her balcony in the Middle East to pray for a specific people group on-site.

I spent many evenings standing on my apartment balcony overlooking the lights of a city of 1 million people. In view were several mosques. My heart would feel heavy, wondering how only two workers would be able to set foot in thousands of homes below.

Night after night I silently watched hundreds of Muslim families go to sleep, thinking they had it all figured out. My heart broke to see how the land where Jesus so often passed through, and many of his disciples invested years of ministry, had turned back to a false god. All I could do in those moments of desperation was pray for randomly chosen lights that I saw, praying that whichever family the light represented would somehow be exposed to the one and only true Light.

I prayed for individuals as they passed by on the street below. I asked God to bestow His truth on a group of men who gathered at the nearby store. I asked Him to give a mother the courage and strength to raise her children to know who their real Father is. And I prayed that the children who played on the street into the late hours of the night would live in a community that had returned to its one true Master. As I voiced my burdens to the Almighty, my feeling of desperation was slowly replaced with a sense of hopefulness and joy.

Whether you pray on-site in a foreign land or pray for specific people in your own community, prayerwalking is a practical way to be focused and alert in prayer. It will change your life!

APPLY IT

1. Read Genesis 5:21–24 and Genesis 6:7–9. What do you think it means to walk with God? What would your life look like if you were walking with God in the way you just described?

2. How did the students' experiences of prayerwalking speak to you?

3. Take a virtual prayerwalk by going to www.thetask.org/students/ G_Passion/prayer.htm, or go on your own prayerwalk in your community to pray for a lost people group.

For further study (optional):
Go to www.thetask.org and click on "spiritual growth" then "prayer." Research how you can adopt a people group or pray for the nations. To find out more about prayerwalking, click on "books on global prayer" and order Follow Me: Lessons for Becoming a Prayerwalker *by Randy Sprinkle.*

CREATE A PRAYER SUPPORT NETWORK

If you are considering going on a student mission trip, you need other people to pray for you. You will likely face difficulties and spiritual warfare as you prepare for your trip and while you are serving on the mission field, so it's vital for you to create a prayer support network.

Ask the Holy Spirit to help you know who should be on your prayer team. Think about students in your campus ministry or church who walk with the Lord daily. Consider people of all ages who are committed to prayer. Ask these people to commit to pray for you for a specific amount of time each day or during a certain day each week. Ask your church family to pray together for you before and during your trip.

Give your prayer supporters a specific list of prayer requests to help direct their prayers for you and the people group you'll be visiting. Your list of prayer requests may include, but not be limited to, the following:

1. Pray that God will glorify Himself through your ministry.

2. Pray for opportunities to share your faith.

3. Pray for boldness as you witness.

4. Pray for God to prepare the hearts of the people you will encounter.

5. Pray for your cultural sensitivity and understanding.

6. Pray for your relationship with your supervisor.

7. Pray for team unity.

8. Pray for your relationships with nationals.

9. Pray for safety in travel and health on the field.

10. Pray for humility and a flexible spirit.

11. Pray for protection from loneliness and depression.

12. Pray for peace of mind for your family in your home country.

13. Pray that God will use your mission experience to create a passion in you for missions.

14. Ask them to continue to pray for you when you return from your trip.

When you commit to take the good news to an area that has limited access to the gospel, you can be sure that the enemy is going to get mean and spiritual warfare will be strong. But you can fight back through prayer!

Esther is an example of someone who asked others to pray for her in a difficult situation. This Jewish teenager had her world turned upside down when Queen Vashti refused to do what her husband, King Xerxes, asked (Esther 1:10–19). The king got really mad and sent the queen away. The king decided he'd find a new wife, so all the beautiful teenage girls were brought to the palace to have makeovers before the king made his choice.

When Esther was taken to the palace, she probably didn't want to leave her kind cousin, Mordecai. The way things turned out, Esther became the chosen one of the king, but more importantly, she was the chosen one of the King of kings. She totally left her comfort zone to follow her Lord for His purpose: to save the Jewish nation from being destroyed.

Esther prepared herself for the king with beauty treatments and special food. During her preparation, Mordecai sent a message to his cousin: "Who knows whether you have not attained royalty for such a time as this?" (Esther 4:14b, NASB). Esther made up her mind to intervene for her people by going to the king, even though it was not lawful to do so without being summoned.

The task was dangerous and Esther knew she would be facing great spiritual warfare, so she created a prayer support network by asking all the Jewish people in the area to pray and fast for her. She had an unwavering faith in God and a love for a people group. That's why Esther said, "If I perish, I perish" (Esther 4:16). God answered prayer, and He saved the Jews from destruction.

God strengthens us to fight the enemy through prayer. Through a prayer support network, you can be part of bringing life to a people group, just like Esther did.

APPLY IT

1. Read Ephesians 6:10–17 and list all the armor pieces that you must put on.

2. Read Ephesians 6:18, 1 Thessalonians 5:17, and Matthew 17:21. How are prayer and fasting crucial to being victorious during spiritual warfare?

3. Read James 4:7 and Matthew 4:10. What are Christians instructed to do?

For further study (optional):
Read Esther 2–8. Think about how evil plans for destruction were thwarted as a result of prayer.

AMAZING RESULTS OF PRAYER

Answered prayer is underrated these days. If something can't be explained by science or logic, then most of the time, people discredit it or call it a coincidence. Yet God still answers prayer today! He continues to work supernaturally in our world and even performs miracles today to encourage Christians, to be a sign for unbelievers, and to bring glory to Himself.

When Jesus performed miracles during His ministry on earth, people were amazed and they praised God. It brings great pleasure to Jesus when He sees people glorifying the Father. When Jesus healed the demon-possessed man in Mark 5:15–20, He told the man to tell his family the great things that the Lord had done for him. When the man told his people group about his miraculous healing, they all marveled and glorified God. In Matthew 15:30–31, many people marveled when Jesus healed the lame, blind, and others—and they glorified God as a result.

God also answered the prayers of the early church. In Acts 16:25–33, we read that Paul and Silas were praying and praising God while in prison, and God suddenly brought an earthquake to open all the prison doors. This led to the jailer's salvation. Peter's friends were praying for his release from prison (Acts 12:5–17), and when Peter showed up at the house, they could hardly believe it!

Sometimes we have a hard time believing in answered prayers, as Peter's friends did. You might think it would be an amazing answer to prayer if your parents approved of you going on a mission trip, or if you raised enough money to go, or if you even decided to go!

Countless students have experienced firsthand God's incredible works in response to prayer. One such student is Teresa from Campbellsville University.

I was given the amazing opportunity to travel to Tanzania. My team and I shared Bible stories to children in a nursery school. During the same time that we were working with the children, the villagers were worried because it had not rained. The local pastor said that they needed only one more rain for their crops. We prayed fervently for rain. After about a week of prayer, it looked as if rain clouds began to roll in. Right before midnight that very night, the rain came. And it continued to rain. We were told that the village of Likamba received more rain than they had seen in nine years. It was unbelievable! God heard the cries of his children, and He answered in abundance.

Another student, Derek from Brazosport College, tells about God's amazing answer to his prayer for an opportunity to share the gospel in a restricted area in Central Europe.

We had been doing a basketball camp for 10- to 15-year-olds. The last day of camp, a couple of kids asked if we would be back that next week, and when we told them no, they all broke into tears. As we walked away, tears welled up in my eyes. I wanted them to know the love of God, a love much greater than I could ever give them. I wanted to turn around and tell them the truth. But I couldn't because it was illegal to witness to a minor.

I began to sob, but God calmed me and said, "**I have sent you to love these kids. Let Me take care of the rest**". For the next hour, I asked Him why I couldn't do it, and if I didn't do it then, how and when? All I heard from Him was **oolu**, which in the native language means "sit." So I sat for about 20 minutes. Then, a young boy came to sit down next to me. He was reading a Bible in his language. He looked at me and had his finger on a verse. Although I didn't know the language, I knew what that passage said because it was John 3:16. I smiled and said, "Jesus loves you and so do I." The child's face lit up, and he ran off telling all the kids that Jesus loved him and so did I. It never fails that God always finds a way.

Another student, April from New Orleans Baptist Theological Seminary, was part of a prayer meeting in Thailand that was similar to Peter's jailhouse experience.

While serving in Thailand, I took a group from America to worship with local Thai Christians. We had a wonderful time worshiping together and meeting new people. There was a refugee family there from Africa that had been living in hard conditions in Thailand for four years. They began to sing African songs, and everyone was enjoying the beautiful sounds. Suddenly they received a call that three of their oldest children had been detained by the authorities. The atmosphere turned from laughter to tears as we all gathered around the family to comfort them.

The Thai pastor called us into a circle and said, "We will pray." We joined hands and each person began praying out loud in their own language. My skin prickled with goose bumps as I heard Thai, French, English, and Japanese voices all praying for this hurting family. We finished praying together and left with the promise to continue to pray. Later that night, we received word that the children had been freed!

Another amazing answer to prayer was witnessed by Jordan from the University of Texas.

We were sitting at a North African coffee shop across from a mosque and praying that someone would come out of the mosque so that we could start a conversation. After the religious prayer time being held there, two guys came to sit right behind us at the shop. We asked if we could sit with them, and we talked about American movies. They mentioned that their favorite movies were from Mel Gibson. We asked if they saw "The Passion," and they said they did but didn't understand why Jesus died. We were able to talk for nearly two hours about Jesus Christ!

Ashley from East Texas Baptist University, another student who went to North Africa, reported this incredible answer to prayer:

Some of our team went with a national brother to prayerwalk in a specific part of town. We prayed that God would reveal Himself to the people and that He would stir up urgency for nationals to know the one, true God. Well, in the middle of a field, we found a little mosque. I immediately felt an urgency to pray. I prayed that the Father would remove the blinders from the leaders' eyes and that the people would know the love and grace of the Father. Two days later, the national brother reported that a man who was highly esteemed at the mosque had become a Christian and burned all his religious books, robes, and prayer mats. There is power in praying!

Never underestimate the power of prayer and God's supernatural works. Even those in heaven sing this song to the Lord: "Great and marvelous are Thy works, O Lord God, the Almighty; righteous and true are Thy ways, Thou King of the nations" (Rev. 15:3, NASB).

APPLY IT

1. Do you believe that God still answers prayer in amazing ways? Why or why not?

2. Read Acts 12:5–17. Do you often pray for something to happen, and then when God answers, you can hardly believe it? Give an example if this has happened to you.

3. Which student story particularly spoke to you in this lesson and why?

For further study (optional):
For deeper prayer preparation, go to www.thetask.org/students/G_Passion/prayer. htm#prayerguides to read a 31-day prayer guide by Nick Lear.

GOD'S CALL: RANDOM OR REAL?

Last week, we learned that every Christian—including high school and college students—can participate in the Great Commission by praying for world missions. This week, we will begin to focus on those students whom God has specifically called to participate in an overseas mission project.

In 2005, more than 7,000 students spent their school break or summer in locations worldwide with the International Mission Board, one of the largest evangelical missions organizations. And God continues to call thousands of students, just like you, to experience what He is doing in the world through short-term volunteer projects or mission service. So how do you know if God is calling you to an extreme adventure of serving Him?

Simon Peter and Andrew were surprised when Jesus unexpectedly appeared while they were fishing and said, "Come, be my disciples, and I will show you how to fish for people!" (Mark 1:17, NLT). Peter and Andrew didn't ask questions; they simply dropped their fishing nets and followed Jesus. In a similar way, you may hear about an international mission trip, and even though you've never thought of serving overseas, you'll decide that God wants you to go.

Natalie from Berea College had a surprising God-moment experience that stirred her heart to participate in world missions.

I will never forget. . . . It was late November, and I was sitting in a crowded room at a banquet on campus. There was nothing religious about the event, not even a prayer before the meal, but I consider that evening to be one of the most important moments of my spiritual journey.

I was enjoying myself, eating exotic food, applauding my fellow students as they performed ethnic dances and songs, and chatting with acquaintances who, like me, appreciated diversity. But in the midst of my contentment, there was a part of me that felt . . . indescribable. In fact, I have decided there is not one word in English that accurately expresses the calling of God.

I thought about the students who were performing. They were studying in a country that allows religious freedom. They were in the heart of the Bible Belt, where stories of Jesus and people who genuinely know Him abound. But what about their families and friends back home? The gospel could not possibly be as easily accessible for those people. And then the realization of it all stirred the depths of my stomach. I was supposed to bring the good news to them. I had been entrusted with the task of making disciples. I was called to go to the nations.

Maybe, like Natalie, you've never considered mission work. Or perhaps you have been thinking that you'd like to go on a mission project. Either way, if God is calling you to be part of student missions, He will find a way to make His call clear to you. Whether you're called in a moment or over time doesn't matter.

Isaiah was called by God to be a messenger. He got excited when God asked, "Whom shall I send, and who will go for us?" Isaiah shouted,

"Here am I. Send me!" (Isa. 6:8). You easily get the picture of Isaiah saying, "Pick me! Pick me!"

God may already be preparing you for your student missions adventure. A student summer worker in North Africa made this observation at the end of his experience:

> On a windy deck of a ferry, watching the sun go down, we left the country. We left behind much of ourselves and, I hope, a fragrance of Christ. You truly know that you are ministering in God's will when a place on a map becomes a place in your heart. This windswept, desert country is certainly one of the harshest lands on earth, but it is so full of unanchored souls, waiting for hope. God is there. He can do a great work. The question is, who will join Him?

Robert from Clemson University was challenged by a church leader while he was a high school student. He said,

> Spending one of my summers during college doing missions work was a decision I made while a freshman in high school. My youth minister does a great job of encouraging all of us to commit one summer of our college years to the Lord.

God is calling all of us to be a part of sharing the good news of Jesus, whether in our own community or overseas. During the next five days, you'll hear from other students who have been in your shoes concerning God's call, look at ways to find out if God is calling you to think internationally, and read about people in the Bible who had to figure out this "call" thing.

GOOSE BUMPS OR GOD'S CALL?

How do you know whether you have a good case of the goose bumps or an actual call from God to be a student missionary? Good question. Perhaps you heard a missionary tell exotic tales of danger and adventure while reaching hundreds of people for Christ. You enjoy survival movies and television programs, so a summer or spring break trip overseas sounds right up your alley. Do tingly feelings mean that you're supposed to buy a plane ticket and pack your bags?

Before you commit to go overseas, take an honest look at your motivation for considering such a trip. Here's an easy way to check your motivation:

I WANT TO GO ON THIS MISSION TRIP BECAUSE:
> (a) *I like the idea of going somewhere exotic, and I have nothing better to do.*
> (b) *A really cute girl/guy has signed up to go.*
> (c) *I feel guilty if I tell the mission trip supervisor no.*
> (d) *I'm highly talented and have a lot to give.*

If you chose any of these answers, you could safely deduce that your motivation for going may be about *you*.

Missions is not about you. And it's not something to be taken lightly. According to pastor and author John Piper, "Christ was on mission to magnify God. ... Jesus came into the world for *God's sake*—to certify *God's* integrity, to vindicate *God's* Word, to magnify *God's* glory. Since God sent his Son to do all this, it is plain that the primary motive of the first great mission to unreached peoples—the mission of Jesus from heaven—was God's zeal for the glory of God." He goes on to say that "a heart for the glory of God and a heart of mercy for the nations make a Christ-like missionary."[4]

Do you really believe that we live in a lost and dying world? Do you desire to obey the Lord's commission to make disciples of all nations by taking the gospel to the world? If so, then perhaps God is calling you to participate in student missions to share the good news of Jesus Christ in a foreign land.

Abram was called by God to go into an unknown land. In Genesis 12, God told Abram, "Go forth from your country, and from your relatives and from your father's house, to the land which I will show you; and I will make you a great nation, and I will bless you, and make your name great; and so you shall be a blessing" (vv. 1–2, NASB). The Bible doesn't say whether Abram was counting his herds of sheep or feeding his goats when God called him. It doesn't say whether Abram got goose bumps or was scared out of his wits when God told him to leave home. However, we can be sure that Abram took God's call seriously. How do we know that? Abram *obeyed*. "By faith Abraham, when he was called, obeyed by going out to a place which he was to receive for an inheritance; and he went out, not knowing where he was going" (Heb. 11:8, NASB).

You will know that your call is real when God compels you to take the steps to obey Him and become a student missionary. It won't be a mountaintop feeling one day that fizzles out the next. If God has called you to participate in student missions, you will be consumed by a passion to follow Him wherever He leads.

Mandy from Yellowstone Baptist College had this to say about her call to be a student missionary:

> As I reflect on the sovereignty of God portrayed in my recent trip to Northeast Asia, I stand in awe at His ability to orchestrate the events of my life in such a way that I could be used as a tool for Him. I surrendered myself to Him, confessing His lordship and pronouncing my obedience to go wherever and whenever He called me. Soon an opportunity arose. I couldn't get it off my mind, so I decided to take the opportunity to go on mission for God. I

left on an adventure to teach in a conversational English camp.

My horizons were expanded as God transplanted me into a city with six times more people than currently reside in my home state of Montana! God opened my eyes to see beyond myself and into the lives of literally millions of people just like me who are in desperate need of His love. God can use us in ways we would never even imagine if we surrender to His call. Responding to God's call is so fulfilling, exciting, and challenging!

Another student, Johnathan from the University of the Cumberlands, didn't have fireworks in the sky when he felt called to missions.

The feeling of God calling me overseas was very subtle. It wasn't the voice of a youth pastor saying, "I really think you should go with us and do construction." For me, it was a longing to go where all I had was God. I didn't want to do a favor for God; what does He need from me? He just wants me to be willing to go, and He'll do the work through me.

Like Mandy and Johnathan, you may have surrendered yourself to obey God wherever and whenever He leads. If God is calling you to participate in student missions, His call may start out as a tingly feeling that you need to check out. If God gives you a passion for world missions and compels you to go, then be like Mandy and Johnathan and follow through with what He is asking you to do.

What if several missions opportunities arise and you feel that God might be calling you to one of them? Which one do you choose? Hopefully, day 3 of this week's lesson will help you answer this question. For the moment, know that the answer won't be on a banner trailing behind an airplane in the sky. God will make the answer clear to you, however, at the right time.

APPLY IT

1. Have you ever felt like God might be calling you to go on a mission trip? If so, explain. If not, explain whether you are open to His leading to go.

2. Can you identify with Mandy or Johnathan? How?

3. Write out a brief prayer in which you surrender your life to whatever purposes God has for you.

For further study (optional):
Read Genesis 12:1–7 and Genesis 15:1–6. When God called Abram, what promises were connected with the call, and what was Abram's response? What can you learn from this?

HOW COME?

Robertson McQuilkin had just finished telling a group of students that billions of people have not heard the good news of Christ but *cannot* hear because so few are willing to tell the unreached. From the back of the auditorium, a voice rang out, "How come?" Dr. McQuilkin responded, "How come, what?" The student asked again, "With so many unreached people, how come so few are going?"

That is a very good question. Dr. McQuilkin came up with the following five answers to the haunting question, "How come so few are going?"

- *We don't care.* Do I love myself so much that I am focused on my own agenda and my own needs? Or do I have such an extreme love for God and an appreciation for His great love for me that I express it through loving the lost?

- *We don't understand.* Do I see the world like God views the world, one that He loves so much that He gave His only Son to die for each person? Or am I so turned off by the differences of others that I forget that God wants them to be saved?

- We *think there must be some other way.* Do I really believe Jesus, who said, "I am the way, and the truth, and the life; no one comes to the Father, but through Me" (John 14:6, NASB). Or do I think that God is going to let everyone into heaven?

- *Our prayer is peripheral.* Am I spending more time praying for my needs rather than for the lost? Or am I praying consistently for God's will to be done on earth as it is in heaven? Am I praying for God's Spirit to send out servants to preach the good news to all peoples?

- *Someone isn't listening.* Do I believe that the Great Commission found in Matthew 28:19–20 is for every believer? Should I be "planning to go, but willing to stay" instead of "willing to go, but planning to stay"[5]?

The Old Testament prophet Jonah didn't want to go to Nineveh. When God told him to go, he went running the other direction. So God had to get Jonah's attention another way. Apparently it took a lot for Jonah to see the light, so He used the fear factor way—a very close encounter with the belly of a big fish and a pretty nasty worm that ate Jonah's shade tree (Jonah 1:17; 4:7).

Natalie from Joliet Junior College said it took her a while to obey God's call for her to go overseas.

Six years ago, I felt a very strong calling to the mission field. I was scared to say yes to God. For me to say yes meant that I would have to be willing to give up my comfort and be willing to go wherever. I fought against this calling because I already had a "great" plan for my life. I was too scared to be away from all the people I loved and all the things I had. Finally, after struggling in my relationship with Him, I told God I would trust Him and go wherever He may lead.

For the past three summers, I have been truly blessed to serve in Bulgaria. God has not only worked in lives of the Bulgarians, but He has also changed my life forever. I have learned what it means to be a true servant of Christ. God has put an excitement in me that cannot be contained. My gift of salvation is not a gift to be guarded but instead one to share.

Notice that Natalie said that ignoring God's call for three years caused her to struggle in her relationship with Him. Not until she gave up her own plans and followed His specific call for her to go overseas, whatever the cost, did she have joy.

Being intentionally distracted from God's plans was a problem for Jonathan from William Carey College.

> We **talk** about poverty, suffering, and spiritual need. We watch television images of places filled with needs, but we feel nothing. We hear a missionary describe some people group, about how desperately they need Christ, and we hurry away to distract ourselves.
>
> This pattern—I am guilty of it more than anyone—comes to mind as I journey through China. And gradually, sometimes suddenly, the depth of people's needs hits me and won't let go because I cannot hide from it here. The reality is impossible to escape, and even though I only understand maybe 10 words of the local language, and I really don't like rice anymore, I cannot help liking these people and maybe even loving them.
>
> I have come to this corner of East Asia to share the gospel and maybe, somehow, understand the gospel more myself and actually live it. God has brought me to love people. I want them to know "for whom Christ died" and for me to be stirred to love with His self-giving, brokenhearted love for all mankind. I pray He will not let me be distracted again.

Are all Christians called to participate in spreading the gospel? Absolutely! Jesus gave all His followers the commission to make disciples of every nation (Matt. 28:19–20). So does that mean you have to get a passport? It's possible. See what God is telling you as you read the next few pages.

APPLY IT

1. If we are all called to participate in the Great Commission, then how come many Christians are not praying for the lost, giving to world missions, or going on mission trips?

2. Are any of the five answers Dr. McQuilkin gave familiar to you personally? If so, which one?

3. What is the difference between being "willing to go, but planning to stay" and "planning to go, but willing to stay"? Which describes your heart attitude?

For further study (optional):
Do you believe that the Great Commission is for all Christians or only for missionaries? Explain your answer, using Scripture, and describe various ways that Christians can participate in the Great Commission.

CONFIRMING YOUR CALL

Going on a student mission trip is not a random decision. Part of preparing to go on a mission trip is being sure that you're doing the right thing. In their book *Experiencing God*, Henry Blackaby and Claude King share at least four ways that God lets us know that we're on the right path: prayer, His Word, other people, and circumstances.[6]

We saw in the first week of this study that God uses prayer. As you listen to God in prayer, He will confirm His call.

Laura from the University of Tennessee began with prayer, and God confirmed His call for her through His Word and circumstances.

> I have been on several mission trips, but all of these trips have been on a team and only for a week. I never considered going somewhere for a whole summer, so when my college pastor challenged me to pray about it, I came up with many excuses why I could not go. However, I did say that I would pray about it.
>
> After praying for a few weeks and not feeling like I had heard from God, I decided to fast and pray about the decision. I had no idea that God would speak to me the way He did. The day I fasted was December 1, which happened to be World AIDS Day. I knew this was not a coincidence since God had given me a heart for AIDS in Africa, and He confirmed His direction for me throughout the day. One of my fears was my parents' reaction, but God led me to Isaiah 51:7, which talks about not fearing the reproach of men.
>
> That same night, I arrived at church to find out that a girl who was going to Africa as a short-term missionary was going to speak to us. It was then that I found out about the possibility of working with her for the summer doing hospital

visits and HIV prevention education in schools. God gave me such a peace that this was where He was leading me to go, and I ended up having the most amazing experience of my life in Africa seeing God at work and being able to join Him.

I have never heard God speak more clearly than when He called me to spend my summer in Botswana. Sometimes God may speak to us in a still, small voice, and other times He may speak to us loud and clear. The important thing is that we are open to hearing His voice and following Him.

Amy from Oklahoma Baptist University also found God's Word to be helpful during her process of deciding to be a student missionary to South America.

As I prayed more, I became certain that God was leading me to Quito. I didn't know what I would do in Quito, which made me nervous. God then showed me Genesis 12:1: "The LORD had said to Abram, 'Leave your country, your people and your father's household and go to the land I will show you.'" Abraham didn't know where he was going, but he still followed God. God reassured me that my summer was in His hands.

God not only speaks to us through prayer and His Word, but He also uses friends and family to give us a message. Kaylin Bowers from Gardner-Webb University had this experience before spending 10 weeks in Poland:

With my stomach in knots, I continued to research possible mission trips for photographers. As I was searching, nothing seemed right. "God, help me find one, please!" I prayed. "You know my desires. Help me to find something where I can serve You and learn, too."

I reminded my collegiate adviser that I wanted to combine missions and photography. "Oh! I know the perfect thing. How about Poland?" An overwhelming peace washed over me, and an unforgettable journey began.

For Abbi from Southeast Missouri State, God used a family to confirm His call for her to go to North Africa.

Planning a trip to North Africa was the last thing I thought I would be doing in my busy sophomore year [in college]. But when a family I had grown up with contacted me from this country asking me to help, the Lord made it very clear that I was to go to North Africa.

Through my brothers and sisters in Christ, I knew that I would make it there with Christ by my side. My student group took up an offering to cover my expenses and lifted me up in their prayers daily. My family donated money and prayer, even though in their hearts they would rather me stay home. My hometown church held a special offering in my name, which raised enough money for my plane ticket and passport.

Through prayer, the Word, circumstances, and family and friends, God is gracious to confirm His call to each of us, showing us whether our part in the Great Commission is to pray, to give financial support, or to go overseas as missionaries. We don't have to rely on feelings, but we can know for sure that the Father wants us to join Him in what He is doing in the world.

Dustin, a graduate student at Columbia International University who has gone on several mission trips, said,

> In America, there are many opportunities for folks to receive Christ, but those dying out in the world plunge into darkness, not because they turned their backs on the Savior, but because they never had the chance to hear. As I finish up my degree in missions, I ask myself, "How do you know you're called to missions?" The answer is simple . . . "The harvest is plentiful, but the workers are few" (Matt. 9:37, NASB).

APPLY IT

1. What are four ways God confirms His call to join Him in His work overseas?

2. Has God used any of these four ways in your own life to confirm His call? Explain.

3. Which of today's student stories especially spoke to you and why?

For further study (optional):
List Scripture references that could help confirm a possible call from God to you to participate in an overseas mission project.

DON'T BE SURPRISED

You've been learning about how God confirms His call to missions. Perhaps God has been using prayer, His Word, circumstances, and family and friends to get your attention, and you are now fairly certain that God is calling you to go on some kind of overseas project. So what now?

Two things are sure to happen to you as you prepare for your mission trip, so don't be surprised. Satan is going to make you doubt yourself and your call; however, God is going to show you how your decision positively affects others and yourself.

Let's look at the situation with Satan first. The Bible tells us that Satan is a liar (John 8:44). He would love to make you doubt whether you have anything to offer as a student missionary. He wants you to focus on yourself and your insecurities, stay in your comfort zone, and be too scared to take such a leap of faith. He will do everything possible to keep you from being involved in missions.

If you plan to be part of a student mission trip, your difficulties will go beyond simply doubting. You may experience a lack of financial support. You might face a family crisis. Or you may be afraid to go. And these are problems you may face *before* the mission project even begins. The enemy wants to zap the joy out of serving God, but don't let him do it.

Satan loves for you to focus on yourself and doubt your abilities. Joey from Oklahoma Baptist University decided to join a student project to East Asia. He said, "I was very scared and felt like I had nothing to offer but the love of Christ." After going on the trip, however, Joey said that his life was changed and that he planned to go on another project.

Jamie from Southern Wesleyan University felt led to go to Brazil, but not without feeling insecure about her abilities.

*I felt this overwhelming pull at my heart and heard God very clearly say, "You are my laborer. . . . Go to the harvest." After a few months of applications and trying to decide where God wanted me, I finally decided on Brazil. At the time I couldn't believe that was where God wanted me because I don't speak **any** Portuguese. But, needless to say, God's plan prevailed because He provided a wonderful woman named Iracema who stayed by my side and translated for me. I was able to share the gospel in schools without being afraid. I can't believe God chose me to go alone to a foreign country to do missions. But my pastor reminded me that God doesn't necessarily call the qualified; He qualifies the called. That's what He did to me, and it changed my life.*

A student from North Greenville University, Joanna, said that she prayed for three months before the name of a specific country in the Pacific Rim flashed across her mind as the place to go on a mission project.

Since I knew nothing about this country, I researched it on Encarta. Everything that I read was what I never wanted. The country was 95 percent Buddhist, it had a difficult language, the people were poor, and the main foods were two of my least favorite. I turned away from the computer, cried, and said, "No, God, I won't do it." My will continued to revolt against God's, and I was left physically, emotionally, and spiritually drained. Finally, after two weeks, I reluctantly submitted and said, "If you make a trip available, I'll go." Less than two months later, I was planning a one-month trip for the summer with a worker in the Pacific Rim.

At the end of my time there, I found myself crying yet again.

This time, however, I was crying because the Lord had allowed me to take part in His work in that country. I was also crying because I wished I had immediately trusted God rather than taking two weeks to submit to His plan. His ways are so much higher and better than my own.

Satan is very clever about how he tries to make us second-guess God's call to serve overseas. He doesn't want you to glorify God or have a heart of mercy for the nations. In fact, Satan wants you to stay comfortable and to doubt that God could ever use you. But don't let him mess with you! This is the moment in which 2 Corinthians 10:5 would be a good verse to have memorized. It says, "We are destroying speculations and every lofty thing raised up against the knowledge of God, and we are taking every thought captive to the obedience of Christ" (NASB). In other words, take those scary, doubtful, and self-absorbed thoughts to jail and throw away the key!

Also, don't be surprised when you see your obedience to follow Jesus on a mission project radically affect others and yourself. Trisha from Boston University had this to say:

The process of getting to India for a mission trip did more for my relationship with Christ than any other single event in my life. I was given the opportunity to speak to my family and friends about why I was going, which led to outwardly sharing and showing my faith with much greater ease and confidence.

People will be interested that you may want to be a student missionary, and many will want to support your efforts. Your act of obedience will often have a positive effect on others.

You will also be personally affected by your obedience to God's call. In fact, once you go, you will never be the same. Kristen in Oklahoma had a life transformation after her overseas mission trip.

> Our team climbed mountains to visit a sacred Buddhist cave. I was amazed at the overwhelming task of presenting the gospel to people who had never heard of Christ. How were we to translate the truth and love of Christ?
>
> Tossing our shoes, we found ourselves in the darkness and cold of the cave. The gold of more than 8,000 Buddha images brought a hush over the place. As we moved, our guide pointed out some of the names inscribed below the statues: "king of kings," "judge of judge," and "the great physician." The glitter of the statues could not dispel the darkness there. Overwhelmed, I found my way out of the cave.
>
> The Lord has a way of bringing conviction and comfort all in the same moment. **This is why you've come, Kristen. This is what I had to show you.** Broken, I could only thank the Lord that Jesus Christ alone is King of kings, Lord of lords, Judge of judges, and the Great Physician. Halfway around the world, He'd graciously brought me to a place to recognize that reality. The calling of the Lord was now inscribed on my heart forever—the good news of Jesus Christ extended to all people.

Count on Satan doing a number on you when you seek to follow Jesus and participate in His commission to make disciples of every nation. And don't be surprised when your obedience affects you and others in positive ways.

APPLY IT

1. What are two things we should expect when following God on a mission project?

2. Write out and memorize 2 Corinthians 10:5.

3. Write out a short prayer to God concerning any doubts, fears, or insecurities you have about serving overseas.

For further study (optional):
Read Matthew 4:1–11. How did Jesus deal with Satan?

TIMING IS EVERYTHING

As amazing as the idea of being a student missionary may seem, it would be useless for you to go unless you know Jesus as the forgiver of your sins and leader of your life. Just as God desires that the nations know Him, He also wants you to know Him. Do you have a personal story of salvation to tell the nations? If you are not sure that you're a Christian, then the first step you need to make is to say yes to God's call on your life to follow Him in repentance. It is important that you speak to a youth leader, college supervisor, or pastor who can help you.

If you are sure that you're a Christian, then you must ask, "Is God calling me, right now, to follow Him on an overseas mission project?" You see, timing is everything. If you are simply "talking the talk" but not "walking the walk" as a Christian, then it would be better for you to develop your relationship with the Lord more deeply through His Word and prayer. Remember, God is looking for young men and women whose hearts belong to Him. "For the eyes of the LORD move to and fro throughout the earth that He may strongly support those whose heart is completely His" (2 Chron. 16:9a, NASB).

Do you feel like you can't see God's plan for you? Take heart in this verse: "I will lead the blind by a way they do not know, in paths they do not know I will guide them. I will make darkness into light before them and rugged places into plains. These are the things I will do, and I will not leave them undone" (Isa. 42:16, NASB).

The Old Testament prophet Jeremiah was unsure when God appointed him to preach the gospel to the nations. Now the word of the LORD came to me saying, "Before I formed you in the womb I knew you, and before you were born I consecrated you; I have appointed you a prophet to the nations". Then I said, "Alas, LORD God! Behold, I do not know how to speak, because I am a youth". But the LORD said to me, "Do not say, 'I am a youth,' because everywhere I send you, you shall go, and all that I command you, you shall speak". (Jer. 1:4–7, NASB)

You do not need to be intimidated because you are young. God will speak through you when He calls you to go to the nations just as He did when He called Jeremiah. He will call you to go at the right time.

Elaine from Murray State University followed God through an overseas mission trip in His timing.

I entered college having been intrigued by international missions most of my life. I was sure that my first college summer would be spent overseas, but a strange thing happened: God told me no. I looked at all the opportunities and felt no call or peace. For three summers, I asked God to send me anywhere, and for three summers, God didn't. My junior year, I heard God whisper in my heart that I would go. He did not give me any details, and I wasn't sure it was His voice, but I was humbled and hopeful.

Then, my senior year, my roommate was planning to go to Thailand. As she spoke of what might be required of her, I thought that I would be afraid to go, and with that fear came a nudge from God: **This is the one.** Still I was uncertain, and I missed the deadline to apply. However, not enough people were going to Thailand, and the leaders were looking for more applicants. God had given me another chance. I talked to my mother, who had peace about this trip. In spite of my fear, I had peace, too. I applied, trusting that God would close the doors if going was not His will. The doors flew open, and His will was confirmed.

God's timing was important for Molly from Austin Peay State University.

I knew I was being called to be a part of another mission trip because I had such a life-changing experience on my first one. Thailand was the country chosen to go and I was excited about Thailand and being part of a team that would share the gospel. God had other plans for me, however. He was calling me somewhere else—a place where my abilities would be put to better use. Thailand was fast approaching, but funding wasn't there. I was sad to inform my campus minister that I couldn't go. Yet I still felt God calling me to be a part of something.

It wasn't much longer before a new mission trip was posted—a trip to Uruguay to teach volleyball and Frisbee to young adults over spring break. I knew this was where God wanted me to go. I was certain that He wanted me here because I've always had a love of sports, and I had just finished taking a Spanish class. I praised God for allowing me to wait on His call. God showed me how to be patient for His timing.

If God is calling you to be a student missionary, He has a perfect time for you to go. When that time is right, *you will know*. Tim Elmore, speaker and president of GrowingLeaders.com, said, "The good news is, you don't have to make those big decisions about your calling in a vacuum."

We've seen four ways God confirms His call—His Word, prayer, circumstances, and family and friends—and you will know what to do at the right time. Scripture backs this up. "Your ears will hear a word behind you, 'This is the way, walk in it,' whenever you turn to the right or to the left" (Isa. 30:21, NASB). Psalm 32:8 says, "I will instruct you and teach you in the way which you should go; I will counsel you with My eye upon you" (NASB).

Confirming whether God has called you to missions is not easy; however, once you recognize His call and choose to follow Him as a student missionary, you will have peace. You may still be unsure about exactly how He will go about raising your support or where He will send you, but this is a time for you to simply trust God.

If you feel God nudging you to go overseas for the summer or a school break, you may be asking, "What now?" The answer is simple: "Say yes." Although your trip may be delayed, having a "yes" attitude to God's call on your life will open the door for you to go when the time is right and if He indeed calls you.

To end this lesson, read what April from Samford University said:

> Obeying God's call to spend my summer in Africa was not an easy decision. I can still see the look on my family's faces when I told them that I felt called to Africa. I can hear some school friends say, "Africa! Isn't there a lot of AIDS there? What if you get sick?" Choosing Africa above what others said was a battle, but when we say yes to God no matter how crazy the task, He will abundantly provide.

If there is something that you feel called to do but you've avoided it or said, "I'll do it sometime before I die," then don't wait. God has created you with special desires in your heart, and holding back on His call can create a life of restlessness. Don't have fear about where you are led; just *do it*. Our God is a God full of love, adventure, passion, and fun! Do you really think that He wants you to sit back and watch life go by without embracing His desires for you?

APPLY IT

1. Which scripture in today's lesson particularly encouraged you and how?

2. Why is "being young" a bad excuse for not going on a mission trip? Write down a few examples of young people in the Bible whom God used.

3. Write a prayer to God concerning His call on your life.

For further study (optional):
Read Jeremiah 1. What specific things did God do to and promise to Jeremiah? Is there a promise that you can apply to your life?

THE TRUST FACTOR

It's not easy to trust someone these days. If you're like most students, you have experienced broken promises firsthand. You may have grown up in a family where you experienced divorce, abandonment, or disillusionment. As a child, you may have known adults who could not be trusted, perhaps even leaders in your school, church, or your own family.

Some students grow up with great role models. However, because so many of us have been disappointed by people, we privately wonder if God can be trusted. You might ask, "Will He let me down, too?" It's a fair question. After all, when we can't count on others to be totally honest and dependable, we may be tempted to have a lack of faith in God, who has the power to control our circumstances.

There are many people in the Bible who had every reason not to trust others. Joseph was thrown in a pit and later sold as a slave by his older brothers (Gen. 37:18–28). Hosea had a wife who committed adultery (Hos. 2:5). Job had some unworthy friends who blamed Job for all his trouble (Job 42:7).

And then there's Thomas. Thomas had given up a lot to follow Jesus, the one he thought was the Messiah. When Jesus was killed, Thomas was disappointed. After Jesus rose from the dead, the following event occurred:

Now Thomas (called Didymus), one of the Twelve, was not with the disciples when Jesus came. So the other disciples told him, "We have seen the Lord!" But he said to them, "Unless I see the nail marks in his hands and put my finger where the nails were, and put my hand into his side, I will not believe it."

A week later his disciples were in the house again, and Thomas was with them. Though the doors were locked, Jesus came and stood among them and said, "Peace be with you!" Then he said to Thomas, "Put your finger here; see my hands. Reach out your hand and put it into my side. Stop doubting and believe." Thomas said to him, "My Lord and my God!"

Then Jesus told him, "Because you have seen me, you have believed; blessed are those who have not seen and yet have believed." (John 20:24-29)

Jesus knew Thomas doubted Him, even after all that they had been through together. He reminded Thomas to trust Him and said that blessings are in store for those who trust in Him without seeing everything.

So what does all this have to do with going on a mission project? As we saw last week, you will most likely experience many doubts about being a student missionary. You might think, *How can I possibly raise that much money? What if my parents hyperventilate about me going? How can I possibly communicate the gospel to people when I don't speak their language? What if I get in a dangerous situation? What kind of abilities do I possibly have to offer? What if I have to eat bugs?*

Jesus wants you to trust Him without seeing the big picture. He wants you to take one step at a time and trust Him to work it all out.

Proverbs 3:5–6 says, "Trust in the LORD with all your heart, and do not lean on your own understanding. In all your ways acknowledge him, and he will make your paths straight (NASB)." Even if others have let you down, God can be trusted. He will be with you, even in an outrageous adventure such as a mission project.

You may not see clearly right now, and you may not have a clue about what He has in store for you. But you can take this to the bank: "Those who trust in the LORD are like Mount Zion, which cannot be shaken but endures forever" (Ps. 125:1).

CHANGING YOUR FOCUS

Our society screams out to us, "Love yourself. Feel good. Be happy. Empower yourself. You deserve it. You have a right." But if we are absorbed with the things right in front of us, the things that make us feel good about ourselves, then how can we reach out to a lost and dying world?

If we want to fully understand how to trust God in all situations, and especially as we participate in fulfilling the Great Commission, then taking the focus off ourselves is necessary. We can never see the love that Jesus has for the whole world unless we do. When we are absorbed with the things right in front of us, the things that make us feel good about ourselves, then we cannot reach out to a dying world.

The apostle Paul helps us to understand the concept of turning our focus away from ourselves and focusing instead on Christ. He says, "I was put to death on the cross with Christ, and I do not live anymore—it is Christ who lives in me. I still live in my body, but I live by faith in the Son of God who loved me and gave himself to save me" (Gal. 2:20, NCV).

Are you free to let go of your own comfort, plans, and possessions for the sake of making God known among the nations? Are you ready to change your perspective from focusing on yourself to reaching out to the world?

Daniel and his friends Shadrach, Meshach, and Abednego ended up in a foreign land. Though they probably would have preferred to stay in their homeland, God in His sovereign plan allowed them to be taken away to Babylon. While they were there, they gained favor with the kings, but trouble lurked around the corner. Because of their faith, Daniel's friends were thrown in a fiery furnace, but they survived unharmed. They didn't even smell like smoke! (Dan. 3:19–30). Daniel didn't fare much better—he was thrown into a pit of hungry lions. But with God's protection, he made it out alive and unharmed (Dan. 6:10–24). These four young men trusted God to take care of them whether they lived or died (Dan. 3:17–18).

If you follow God's call to be a student missionary, you may or may not experience persecution. However, you will certainly make sacrifices, especially in the area of denying selfish desires.

Chris from the University of the Cumberlands learned what it meant to deny self as he served as a short-term missionary.

> I learned about a mission trip to France, and God almost immediately laid a desire on my heart to go. I later went through a hectic time and began to question whether I should go overseas. God stepped in to reassure me while I read "My Utmost for His Highest." I realized that it may be appealing for me to stay and do my own thing over the summer, but what God had planned was worth so much more than that.
>
> The summer was not always easy—it was an amazing experience—but there were hard times as well. My grandmother died a few weeks after I got there. I felt alone at times, even with the team by my side, but I learned more reliance on God. God was faithful to grow me in ways I couldn't have imagined, but it still **wasn't about me**. At the end of the summer, I saw how God used nine college students to impact people from France and 37 other countries with His love.

Chris chose not to do his own thing because "what God had planned was worth so much more than that." Although the mission experience caused him to grow, he still said that the trip wasn't about him. In other

MY LIFE, HIS MISSON

words, Chris took the focus off himself and his desires. He trusted the Lord as he abandoned his own plans for the summer.

A student from Louisiana Tech, Aurelia, denied comfort daily while serving in the Philippines. She relates this story:

My summer wasn't easy, and it wasn't even exactly what I wanted to do. I applied to be on a team that traveled to different islands sharing the gospel through drama and sports. But I received an e-mail before leaving stating that they needed people to join a different team. So, in a complete change of plans, I went to Camiguin Island and spent the whole summer hiking and sharing the gospel door - to - door. It was a hard task, because building relationships with people through a translator is hard enough, but then going to a new village day by day made it nearly impossible.

I learned to depend on God's strength to make it through the day. As I washed my clothes by hand, munched on bread, and took bucket baths, I was reminded of how blessed my life was. But there were times of intense struggle as I fought battles spiritually, emotionally, and physically. My prayer every night was, "God, I don't want this, but I want to want this. Please change my heart."

These frustrations are natural in the middle of most any mission project where you're working and not seeing results. But then you meet that person who changes your whole perspective. For me, the person was Ate Palma. She was a Mormon who usually refused to listen to other perspectives on religion. But she was drawn to me and my teammate because she had lost two daughters.

After a week of Bible studies and relationship building, Ate Palma accepted Christ and was baptized along with three others in her family. After passing out thousands of tracts, hiking hundreds of miles, and seeing few responses, one woman's response to the gospel helped me quit struggling and surrender to God's will once and for all.

In his book *Let the Nations Be Glad*, John Piper made a profound statement about self-sacrifice in missions: "I have learned that the way of love is both the way of self-denial and the way of ultimate joy. We deny ourselves the fleeting pleasures of sin and luxury and self-absorption in order to seek the kingdom above all things. In doing so we bring the greatest good to others, we magnify the worth of Christ as a treasure chest of joy, and we find our greatest satisfaction."[7]

Trusting God and denying self may not come easy, but God is worthy to be trusted. He keeps His promises. The way of ultimate joy is in your reach. If you have determined that He is calling you to serve overseas for a time, then trust Him to prepare you to go and to lead you as you serve. Seek His will, and put aside your own will.

Jesus commands His followers to go into all the world, then He reminds us, "I am with you always, even to the end of the age" (Matt. 28:20b, NASB).

APPLY IT

1. Reread Paul's words in Galatians 2:20, and read Galatians 5:24 and Colossians 3:2–3. Which Scripture reference concerning self-denial especially spoke to you and why?

2. When do you find it difficult to trust God?

3. Underline statements in the stories by Chris and Aurelia in which they turned from their own desires to trusting God.

For further study (optional):
Read Daniel 3:19–30 and Daniel 6:10–24. Write down thoughts about the courage of these young men who trusted the living God.

No TURNING BACK

As you seek to trust God and to follow His call to participate in student missions, your faith will be tested. Let's look today at what it means to have a faith that does not look back but goes forward instead.

Under very difficult circumstances, Marsha from Blue Mountain College had to make a choice about following God wherever He led. Once she decided, there was no turning back, and God blessed her as a result.

I was starting at a new school in the fall and desperately needed to work for the summer, find a place to live, get my things together. If ever there was a time to stay home, it was now. But I knew this was my test of faith. I jumped . . . and I landed on the greatest team of island-hopping summer missionaries I could ever have imagined.

When reading through the position papers, I had casually passed over the church-planting positions, because that was definitely not my expertise. But when the assignment came, you guessed it—church planting. Although I was afraid and had no clue where to start, I walked down the streets in Bohol, Philippines, with my teammates, and by the end of the summer, we were sharing with complete ease.

I would be lying to say that was the last "test" I had that summer. However, by the end of the summer, I saw souls whose eternities were at stake. I found greater faith than I have ever known. I found a faithful God who deserves our **complete** *trust. And the place where I was hesitant to go, I was now hesitant to leave.*

Marsha found greater faith than she had ever known, and she also found a faithful God who deserves complete trust. And that's what God wants from you: your complete trust. He wants you to trust in Him with *all* your heart.

In Genesis 22:1–14, God tests Abraham's trust in Him. He tells Abraham to take the most precious thing to him—his only son, Isaac—and offer him as a sacrifice. God had promised Abraham that He would make a great nation from his descendants, and Isaac was his only legitimate child. Abraham believed God's promise. When Abraham, Isaac, and the servants got to the mountain, Abraham said to the servants, "Stay here with the donkey, and I and the lad will go yonder; and we will worship and *return* to you" (Gen. 22:5, NASB; emphasis added). There is no doubt Abraham believed that God would either provide another sacrifice or that He would raise Isaac from the dead (Heb. 11:17–19).

After God provided a ram to sacrifice in place of Isaac, Abraham named the place Jehovah Jireh, which means "The LORD Will Provide." God allowed Abraham to demonstrate complete, extreme trust. Although Isaac may have been scared to death, he got an unforgettable, clear picture of his father's trust in God.

God is calling all of His followers to completely trust in Him. Trusting in Him always requires a sacrifice. That sacrifice involves laying our own desires, our own plans, and our own comfort on the altar.

A student from Gardner-Webb University, Bethany, committed to sharing the gospel in Moldova and North Africa and the Middle East on separate overseas projects.

There is no true satisfaction in anything other than sharing with others the joy that they can receive through Jesus. When in Moldova sharing God's love with orphans, I first heard the call of Christ on my life for full-time missions. At that time, I didn't understand what God was going to do with me, where I would be, or who I would be serving. About two years after Moldova while on a trip to North Africa and the Middle East, God confirmed the call on my life to full-time, overseas missions.

When the difficult times came overseas, it was easy to start to question what I was doing there, but every time, God would provide what I needed, whether it was a scripture I read, hugs from children who desperately needed to hear that they are important, an e-mail from home telling me they were praying for me, or just a cool breeze at the warmest part of the day.

I praise God that "because of the LORD's great love, we are not consumed, for his compassions never fail. They are new every morning; great is your faithfulness" (Lam. 3:22-23).

God is faithful. He is pulling for you. He's on your team. In fact, He's the coach. Don't turn back when you head for the goal, even when you have to make sacrifices along the way. Run to win! The author of Hebrews encourages us to "lay aside every encumbrance and the sin which so easily entangles us, and let us run with endurance the race that is set before us, fixing our eyes on Jesus, the author and perfecter of faith" (12:1–2, NASB).

Jesus Himself never lost sight of where He was headed, and He made the ultimate sacrifice. Trust God and don't turn back.

APPLY IT

1. Read Genesis 22:1–14. Explain the kind of trust that Abraham had in God.

2. What sacrifices did Marsha and Bethany make, and how did they demonstrate a no-turning-back kind of faith?

3. Write a prayer asking God to give you a no-turning-back kind of faith in Him and His purposes.

For further study (optional):
Think of a time when you saw God's faithfulness to you or to someone you know. Write out a personal statement of how God is faithful in Scripture and/or in a personal example.

MY WEAKNESS, HIS STRENGTH

Last week, you read that the prophet Jeremiah was scared when God called Him to be a prophet to the nations. He told God that he didn't know what he could possibly say to others because he was young. But God told him not to worry because He would show Jeremiah where to go and what to say.

You probably can identify with Jeremiah. You may be thinking about participating in a mission project or actually planning to go, but you feel insecure about your abilities. Good! If you think you have something to offer the world, then frankly, God may not want to use you yet. The mission field doesn't need people who have an attitude that says, "I'm going to save the world because I'm so good at it." God uses those who don't rely on their own strength but who will solely rely on Him.

Brooke from the University of West Georgia understood what it meant to rely on God and not herself while serving in Mexico.

People always say that it's not the best idea to tell God what you are and are not going to do, and they sure are right. When God tells us in Jeremiah 29:11 that He has some great plans for us, He is not saying, "Hey, here are some good ideas for life. Take them or leave them." God's plans for us are His will—His good, pleasing, and **perfect** will.

My junior year of college is definitely a testimony to this. I never had any desire to go on a mission trip. I was perfectly content with staying in the same place all of my life. God, on the other hand, did not want me to stay comfortable. That year I ended up in Puebla, Mexico, for a spring break mission trip. After that week my life was never the same.

I had planned to be a teacher since I was five years old. So when I graduated, what else would I do but teach? Well, I wasn't sure, but God definitely knew. He had planned for me to end up back in Puebla, Mexico. The first week was pretty hard. God reminded me that He had me there for a reason and He would always be with me. There were so many times I needed peace, and He never failed to provide it. Many days I would be discouraged that I was useless because of the language barrier.

My friend encouraged me by sending the passage 2 Corinthians 12:9-10. It says, "My grace is sufficient for you, for my power is made perfect in weakness. Therefore I will boast all the more gladly about my weaknesses, so that Christ's power may rest on me. That is why, for Christ's sake, I delight in weaknesses, in insults, in hardships, in persecutions, in difficulties. For when I am weak, then I am strong." God also reminded me that He just calls us to go and tell. Sometimes we are part of bringing in the harvest, but many times we are planting a seed. Regardless of which, the important thing is that the lost are hearing the gospel.

God really changed me. I know that being away from my family, friends, and out of my comfort zone made me fully realize how great He is.

Brooke did not focus on her own abilities, but rather on the strength that God gave her to teach in Mexico. Although she was discouraged, she was comforted by God's Word. She was reminded that when she is weak, she is strong in Christ's power. Likewise, we will never be able to accomplish God's will in our lives if we focus on what *we* can do for

God. Rather, He will release His great power through us when we yield to His leadership and depend on His strength.

Sometimes God allows us to be in situations where we are forced to depend upon His strength. Erin from Shorter College experienced God's strength after an injury while participating on a mission project involving sports.

> As we went from village to village in Moldova, my team and I were promoted as the "American soccer team." In foreign cultures, they don't just play soccer; they demolish anything in their paths. So there I was, in all my American glory, having a blast when the dreaded happened—I severely twisted my knee. Sitting on the side of the field and trying to ease pain, I immediately felt all alone. I was surrounded by Romanian-speaking people, thousands of miles away from home, and I began questioning God. Obviously I was not on this trip for sports.
>
> I am thankful God redirected my path, because if He had not, I would have missed out on so many blessings. I focused the rest of my trip on working with crafts, allowing me to make numerous relationships with people. I was also able to help lead worship during some of the services. Through this, He was my physical strength during my time of weakness, which confirmed my faith and confidence in Him.

A student from the University of Georgia, Christa, also learned about depending on God's strength while overseas.

> A group of 24 people, some medical, some teachers, some sportsmen,

and even a hairstylist, learned the essence of depending on Him in Asia. Though we were only in this country for 10 days, those 10 days were exhilarating and grueling. We were in scorching heat, doing backbreaking work, and we were short on oxygen because we were 11,000 feet above sea level.

Each day the basketball team would teach clinics to the village children, mix cement to build a new wall, and then play games against the men in the area. We could not do this without the strength of the Lord. Before every game, we would have our team huddle under the basketball goal, and we would pray that His strength would be made perfect in our weakness. The supernatural power of our mighty God allowed victories for His kingdom.

We never knew how God was going to use us, because in Asia, the plans always seem to be changing. But we did learn about trusting in Him.

Being willing to trust God, to rely on His strength, is the secret to being free to minister to others. God wants a humble person who is willing to follow His voice. God doesn't need you in all your glory to win the world. He desires you in all your weakness to glorify Him.

APPLY IT

1. Even if you read Jeremiah 1 in "For further study" last week, read again Jeremiah 1:1–10. How can you apply these verses to your life?

2. Underline phrases in the three student stories that spoke to you.

3. What do you think it means to rely on God's strength? What scripture would support your answer?

For further study (optional):

Read Exodus 3:1–14. What was Moses concerned about, and what was God's response? What can you learn from this?

THREE KINDS OF STUDENTS

Student mission volunteers usually fall into three categories when they arrive on the field:

(1) those who are far too confident in their own abilities,

(2) those who are extremely insecure in their abilities, and

(3) those who have God-given skills, a teachable spirit, and a dependence on God's strength.

Needless to say, a missionary would prefer to work with the third kind of student. However, God can totally change overconfident and underconfident students during a mission trip. God lovingly brings His children to proper humility.

Pride is destructive. It always comes from a self-absorbed heart. Whether a person thinks too much of himself or too little of himself, the root problem is pride. "Woe to those who are wise in their own eyes and clever in their own sight," says the prophet Isaiah (5:21). The category one student arrives on the field thinking he personally will change the world. He believes that he has a foolproof plan and that hundreds will be saved because of his efforts, talents, and zealous evangelism. It would be nice if God would get on board with him, but not to worry, the student thinks that he has everything under control. This student will be exhausted in no time flat during an overseas experience. You cannot rely on your own strength and abilities and be in God's will.

Kristi from the University of Miami experienced this truth while serving on an overseas mission project.

Throughout the summer in South Asia, the Lord provided me with the scriptures needed to get through rough times. One morning, I was reading Psalm 51. In the first part, David is pleading for forgiveness. I realized how often I doubt God's sovereignty and His goodness. I, too, began crying out to God to forgive my faithless heart. Sometimes I forget just how powerful our God is and what He is capable of doing.

In verses 10-12, David is asking God for the fortitude to endure trials. I am so quick to get worn out from doing God's work when I am not fully relying on Him. David asks God to renew a steadfast and willing spirit and to restore his joy. My daily prayer became that God would renew me so that I could magnify His glory among the nations.

Finally in verses 13-19, David seeks God's favor. He does this by singing of His righteousness and declaring His praise (vv. 14-15). He recognizes that God loves a broken and contrite heart. I knew in that very moment what God was doing in my heart. I recognized that it was in my brokenness that I really sought God's favor. I came before Him with a heart of humility, pleading for His mercy.

God brought Kristi to a point in which she had to decide that she could not rely on her own abilities or power. She asked God to forgive her and to renew her. Then she humbled herself and began to glorify Him. Kristi's pride disappeared, and God used her.

Pride is not just with the overconfident. Pride also hides in the insecure person. In reality, the insecure person does not trust God enough to mold him into something useful for the kingdom. Students who arrive at their international destination with these insecurities and *remain* like this will be fearful, uninvolved, and extremely homesick. Yet God can change this student if he is willing.

Maryem from Western Kentucky University felt insecure in who she was and how God could possibly use her. However, she was able to see God's purposes for her while volunteering overseas.

I was exploding by a simple prayer for the Lord to tune my heart to His heartbeat. My world was turned upside down, and I found myself on my way across the world. I had grown up in a Muslim household in America and was redeemed by God's amazing intervention in my life at the age of 16. My father and mother were born and raised in Iran; however, I never saw myself as an "international." I had grown up doubting myself and not loving myself as God created me.

Not until my calling to South Asia to work with Muslim women for a summer did I see that God knew what He was doing the whole time. In Psalm 139, God says that He has ordained all my days. It wasn't a surprise to God that I was going to India, and I learned that He had crafted me with my skin tone, hair color, specific gifts, and personality for His glory.

I was sitting in a house of a young Muslim woman when I saw God's divine plan unfold before my eyes. The languages I grew up learning were English and Farsi. Out of the hundreds of dialects spoken in this South Asian country of 1.1 billion people, God perfectly placed me in a city in which their dialect derived somewhat from Farsi. So while I was sharing the gospel with a family without Christ, God used the little Farsi I knew, my background, and my physical makeup to grant me favor and the chance to share the gospel to people who had never heard.

God graciously showed Maryem that He could use her, and she saw for the first time that He had created her for a kingdom purpose. As Christians, we are a part of God's purposes for the world. When we realize that truth, we are free to be all that He wants us to be.

Amy, a teenager from Oregon, found purpose on a mission trip to South America.

> As a 13-year-old, I wanted to go on mission to Brazil, but I wondered how I could talk to people about purpose when I wasn't sure of my own. Then I met my parents' missionary friends. As they shared many stories about how the Lord had moved in the world, I was fascinated. When I went to Brazil, He gave me purpose to do everything I could to bring glory and honor to One who's deserving and to share the hope He's given me with everyone.

God can change the hearts of students who put their focus on Him rather than their own abilities or lack of abilities. Ray from the University of Tennessee at Knoxville learned that God could use his soccer skills in Peru.

> This summer, I noticed how God took unconventional things in my life and used them to further His kingdom. My love for the game of soccer really helped me to connect with the people and opened up many doors for witnessing.

A student from Francis Marion University, Magan, saw a trip to Cuba as one of God's opportunities for her.

I was about to face one of the biggest opportunities of my life. God had led me to Cuba, but I didn't know why, what I was going to do there, or how God would move in the hearts of the Cubans or even me. I was no longer in control of the situation. Could I even make a difference?

During our stay there, we worked with a house church. One of the girls who lived at that house was not a Christian until our leader intentionally asked her questions. She began to cry, and I had never seen the Holy Spirit physically work in someone like that before. I remember her saying, "I have nothing to put my hope and trust in," and at that point, I knew why I came to Cuba. I came to show her Jesus.

We also did a ladies' ministry, baseball ministries, kids' clubs, and street evangelism, none of which I had **ever** done before, but God gave me the words when I needed them.

Do you desire to be a student who uses God-given skills, has a teachable spirit, and trusts God's strength alone? Then be active from this day forward in worshiping and praising the Father (Rev. 4:11), and take Jesus' advice to the disciples found in Mark 9:35: "If anyone wants to be first, he must be the very last, and the servant of all."

APPLY IT

1. Which of the three categories of students are you? Be honest.

2. Read Revelation 4:11 and Mark 9:35. What are the two things that will help you to become a category three student?

3. Write a prayer, praising God, confessing pride if necessary, asking for forgiveness, and asking Him to make you usable, teachable, and filled with His Spirit.

For further study (optional):
Find three verses in Scripture that warn against pride in addition to the ones mentioned in this lesson.

TAKING THE FIRST STEP

This week's lessons have centered on trusting God as you put away self-focus, trusting Him without regrets like Abraham, depending on His strength as you live by the Spirit, and becoming a student who serves without pride. You probably haven't mastered these traits yet. But as you live by God's Holy Spirit each day and choose to focus on Jesus and not yourself, you will become more like Him. To accurately represent Jesus in your own life will do much for the kingdom of God. And as Richard Ross, popular speaker and author, said, "Students want the power and wisdom of God so that they can expand the kingdom."

Faith is trust in our heavenly Father. It's like the old movie in which Indiana Jones seeks the Holy Grail. He has almost found it, but first he must cross a chasm. A bridge is there to safely cross the deep recesses below, but Indiana can't see it. It won't appear until he actually steps out in faith, risking his very life to get to the prized possession. When he takes the first step, he is momentarily shocked that the bridge appears, but then he rushes over the chasm to the other side.

Obeying the Great Commission takes faith—blind faith. You won't know fully what you're getting yourself into. However, at some point you will have to take the first step. As you step out in faith, you can be encouraged by Psalm 9:10: "Those who know your name will trust in you, for you, LORD, have never forsaken those who seek you." God is always going to be with you on your journey of faith.

Alvin from Union University tells about taking that first step of trusting God on a mission project:

That first mission trip can be a very scary thing. I had never been out of the country before, and I was a nervous wreck. For the first time in my life, I was ripped out of my comfort

THE TRUST FACTOR

zone. And it was great! I learned to depend on God in a whole new way, and it did wonders to our relationship. I grew so much after learning how to lean on God.

I tell people that it was almost as if God was waiting for me when I got off of the plane in Guatemala for my first mission trip. I had known Him, but I did not require Him. After I learned that I needed to **need** Him, I spent the next year drawing closer to Him. By my second mission trip, I was much more at ease. We had gotten so much closer that I always felt His presence. This made it so much easier to go to the places that He wanted me to go.

I no longer have a "comfort zone." God's presence in my life has broken down these barriers. As long as I am focused on God and His will for my life, I know that I can do anything He desires.

Alvin's relationship with God changed drastically as a result of a step of obedience. As Alvin focused on God and His will, he could join the apostle Paul in saying, "I can do all things through Him who strengthens me" (Phil. 4:13, NASB).

Another student, Jessica from Dyersburg State Community College, also had to take that first step to participate in an overseas project.

God had placed China on the heart of my collegiate minister, who asked some of us to pray about going to China for Christmas. My first thought was no! I knew all about China, Hudson Taylor, Gladys Aylward, and Voice of the Martyrs. China is dangerous! I didn't want to go. As these thoughts raced through my mind, I heard God say, "**I didn't ask you if you wanted to go. I asked, "Are you willing to go?"**"

81

I had never stepped foot on a plane, but I decided to embark on one of the biggest adventures of my life. Along with my team, I got to present the gospel to deaf-blind individuals. We also went to many different schools and shared the Christmas story. Going to China allowed me to see that wherever God takes me, I know that He will take care of me. I saw how bold our Chinese Christian partners were even in the face of persecution. God showed me how awesome it is to share His love.

Here's the main idea, plain and simple: once you have confirmed God's call for you to go overseas, at some point, you have to stop discussing the possibility of going on a mission trip and just do it. As Alvin and Jessica both experienced, you may have fear when you take that step of faith. But if you truly believe that God is calling you to be a student missionary, then go for it!

APPLY IT

1. Write out and memorize Philippians 4:13.

2. Which student story in today's lesson spoke to you the most and why?

3. Fill in the blanks from the text: "But as you _____ by God's _____ _____ each day and focus on _____ and not yourself, you will become more and more like ____."

For further study (optional):
Summarize in a paragraph what you learned about trusting God in this chapter.

FLEX or FREAK OUT?

You have a choice every day to be flexible and open to what God wants to teach you or to be totally frustrated when things don't go your way. A mission experience is the perfect opportunity to learn how to "go with the flow."

Sometimes a change of plans occurs during mission trips because of unforeseen challenges or incomplete preparation. Other times, despite having the best of human plans, missionaries can be confronted by circumstances that are completely out of their control, such as a change in government policies or a natural disaster.

No matter the source of the challenge while on a mission project, you must choose how you will respond to the change. To have the best possible experience as a student missionary, you must be flexible and adjust to the new circumstances, knowing that the change of plans is no surprise to God, who works out all things according to His will and in His timing.

Stella of Jacksonville State University had a lot to say about what she learned about flexibility when school officials caused a change in her plans. Let's allow her story to introduce this chapter.

Flexibility. That's a good word when you are considering missions. But to be honest, you have to be fluid. God has things planned that we could never imagine. My first trip was to East Asia two summers ago to teach English as a Second Language to college students. We were told that the students would already know English; we were just going to fill in the gaps in their conversational English.

Before I even left the States, the school I would be teaching in changed three times. The last school change was just a few days before I left. Every change was a change of teams as well. I applied for my visa. I got the wrong one. "Be flexible," I told myself. "This is God's plan, not yours." My second visa was delayed. It arrived two days before I left.

We arrived in the country and were on the way to the school when we were told by the school official that we would not just be teaching college students. The school had done such a good job promoting the program that they had around 350 students wanting to take the class. My class was ages 5 to 13. None of them spoke any English. Not a problem . . . we had teacher's assistants (TAs) who would translate for us. Class started, but my TA would not translate for me. She said it was an English class, and we should only speak English. It was no longer time to be flexible—it was time to be fluid. On the days when I was tempted to be frustrated, I reminded myself of what I was really there to do. I was not there just to teach English; I was there to teach them Jesus.

When it was time once again to apply for summer missions, I applied to go back to East Asia. I did everything in my power to go back to the same school. Nevertheless, I got an e-mail saying that my team was being reassigned to another school. When my team got to the new school, we found out that we would be teaching middle school students. When the classes started, we discovered the students could not speak English. We were also not going to have any TAs with us. All I could do was laugh. God, in His wisdom that I could not understand the summer before, had prepared me for this trip.

Because I was fluid in my prior experience, God was able to teach me things that I would need for my next mission trip. We were able to not only teach these students English; we were able to share Jesus. Seeds were planted that will later be watered by students just like you. Don't ever be afraid of where God wants to send you.

OUT OF MY COMFORT ZONE

Life is pretty good, especially if you have your own bed, own transportation, favorite foods, and enough money to live on comfortably. It's when we get out of our comfort zone that we begin to squirm. Yet squirming is good for us because it gives us a chance to build endurance and spiritual maturity (James 1:2–4).

It seems that the apostle Paul faced a change of plans wherever he went as a missionary. He was constantly out of his comfort zone. God made it clear right from the beginning of Paul's ministry that Paul would suffer (Acts 9:15–16). Paul committed to share the gospel in a place where Christ was not known (Rom. 15:20–21), so he learned to be flexible and content whenever he encountered difficulties.

In Philippians 4:11–13, Paul says, "I have learned to be content in whatever circumstances I am. I know how to get along with humble means, and I also know how to live in prosperity; in any and every circumstance I have learned the secret of being filled and going hungry, both of having abundance and suffering need. I can do all things through Him who strengthens me" (NASB).

Margaret, a high school student in Ohio, learned a valuable lesson about being content with what we have while on an international mission trip:

> When I was a freshman in high school, I went on my first international mission trip to Ecuador. While we were in Ecuador, I realized for the first time that God really is everywhere. He is in Ecuador the same as He is in America. In America we are blessed more than we can really ever know, and it was life changing to realize not everyone has as much stuff as we do, but they are equally if not far more

happier than we are. Being content with what we have is hard for us but definitely a lesson God teaches everyone who goes to serve.

As a student missionary, you may face sleeping in a hammock or on the floor, Montezuma's revenge (if you don't know what this is, you don't want to know), language deficiencies, not enough supplies, pit toilets, bugs, sweltering heat, frigid temperatures, and countless other inconveniences. During these times, you can be encouraged by Paul's words in 2 Corinthians 4:16–18: "Therefore we do not lose heart. Though outwardly we are wasting away, yet inwardly we are being renewed day by day. For our light and momentary troubles are achieving for us an eternal glory that far outweighs them all. So we fix our eyes not on what is seen, but on what is unseen. For what is seen is temporary, but what is unseen is eternal."

What kinds of difficulties did Paul face on his missionary journeys? Certainly more than not having air conditioning during his travels. He was beaten, imprisoned, stoned, and shipwrecked; he faced all kinds of danger; he experienced hunger, thirst, sleeplessness, and exposure to the weather; and he lived with constant concern for new believers (2 Cor. 11:23–28).

The struggles most student missionaries face don't come close to Paul's, but the difficulties are real all the same. Jennifer from High Point University understands about leaving comfort behind. After her mission experience, she said,

Breaking out of my comfort zone, being spontaneous, and going to a foreign country without knowing anyone are three things that scare me. God has a way of putting us in situations where

things are not how we would have them by any stretch of the imagination, yet once we're there, He provides for us and we get to experience Him in a whole new way.

I had the blessing of traveling to Swaziland with 17 other college students and adults. We camped in one of the villages for 10 days. We truly experienced how the Swazi people live, and we were honored by their hospitality. God used this experience to reveal how selfish and spoiled I really am.

Through it all, God had a plan, and my life will never be the same.

Did you notice what getting out of her comfort zone did for Jennifer? It built spiritual character. God revealed to her some attitudes that she needed to change, and she did.

James from Angelo State University was stretched spiritually and emotionally in Romania.

Missionaries had warned us about Romanian pastors **always** making you preach if you go to their churches, but I didn't expect it to be true. Let me tell you, it was more than true. It was all a joy, but during my trip, I was asked to preach at four village church services and one funeral. Sounds pretty fun, right? Well, it was! It was also exhausting. Even with all of this, the experience was extraordinary!

James was exhausted, but the challenge was enjoyable. He made a choice to "rejoice in the Lord always" (Phil. 4:4).

Being overwhelmed with vague plans caused initial concern for Bethany from the University of Tennessee, Chattanooga, who served in Peru.

My teammates and I had only been in Vilcashuaman for three days. Our plan was to find out if there were legitimate evangelical churches, follow up with those who had received Christ a few days prior, witness door-to-door, and try to find ways to develop friendships with schoolchildren, despite our team having a limited amount of Spanish. We thought, **Where can we start?**

God immediately sent us Luis, a 14-year-old boy with a desire to know the truth. He came to us with questions about philosophy, evolution, and religion. They were tough questions for which we didn't have eloquent answers, but by the wisdom of the Holy Spirit and through Scripture, Luis understood and believed. We had limited use of the Spanish language, but God's Word proved to be much more powerful than any of his doubts and our lack of a clear plan. Through that one contact, we were able to share the gospel with countless students.

Romans 8:28 promises, "God causes all things to work together for good to those who love God, to those who are called according to His purpose" (NASB). God will allow things to happen in your life to give you an opportunity to become more like Christ. When you participate in overseas missions, you can count on being out of your comfort zone! But you can also count on God using that experience for good, both in your own life and in the lives of those whom you are serving.

APPLY IT

1. Have you ever felt out of your comfort zone concerning something that God asked you to do? If so, how did you grow spiritually as a result?

2. As a student missionary, how should you react when things don't go as planned or the way you prefer? Support with Scripture.

3. What fruit of the Spirit listed in Galatians 5:22–23 would you like to improve in your life? How might these character traits be strengthened on a mission experience?

For further study (optional):
Read Philippians 1 and 2. What do you learn about joy in these two chapters?

CROSS-CULTURAL EXPERIENCES

Most people of the world do not think or live like we do. There are thousands of people groups, and each has its own unique culture. Should missionaries barge in and try to reach people for Christ using methods familiar to them but unacceptable in that culture?

For instance, using beaded witnessing bracelets would actually hinder the gospel in many cultures. Beads and leather strands around a wrist can be interpreted as a charm that invites ancestral spirits to protect or enter a person. That's why it is important to be aware of cultural taboos.

The apostle Paul had a lot to say about witnessing to other cultures. "Though I am free and belong to no man, I make myself a slave to everyone, to win as many as possible. To the Jews I became like a Jew, to win the Jews. To those under the law I became like one under the law (though I myself am not under the law), so as to win those under the law. To those not having the law I became like one not having the law (though I am not free from God's law but am under Christ's law), so as to win those not having the law. To the weak I became weak, to win the weak. I have become all things to all men so that by all possible means I might save some. I do all this for the sake of the gospel, that I may share in its blessings" (1 Cor. 9:19–23).

The apostle Paul had many cross-cultural experiences during his mission trips. When he was in a new place, he took in his surroundings and observed the people. For example, while in Athens, he noticed many idols. When he spoke before a crowd, he started with an observation familiar to the Greeks—the fact that they were religious and that they even had an altar dedicated "to an unknown God." Then Paul explained that he knew this unknown God, the Creator of all things. He even quoted Greek poets who referred to God. He briefly introduced Jesus, without disclosing His name, and taught more to those who were interested (Acts 17:16–34). Paul was a master in relating the gospel to all kinds of people.

A student from Berea College, Joanna, learned to see the world through the eyes of other cultures.

As a student missionary, I had the incredible opportunity to travel to three different countries and share the gospel in a variety of ways. In Poland, I taught puppet workshops at an English camp and helped repair a church building in a town with very little evangelical influence. In Bolivia, I ministered in a rural village. In Thailand, I spent two months teaching English to Buddhist college students.

Our God does not move in the same way in every country. I have learned to be open-minded—as cliché as that sounds—and to always expect more from Him than anything I could dream up on my own. Because of an expanded worldview, I no longer see the world through the eyes of a Protestant girl from Georgia. I now see it through the eyes of a teenage Polish girl, a Guarayu girl in a South American village, and a Thai college student wondering if any of life's answers are to be found in Buddhism. These are people Jesus died for.

If you have never been outside of your own country, you may experience culture shock when you encounter another culture. Karen, a student from Howard Payne University, was shaken when she visited some caves in North Africa.

We hiked down into the caves where the Muslim Africans make sacrifices and pray. Since most are too poor to make a trek to Mecca, coming to the caves is their substitution. When we were finished walking through the caves, the Africans did traditional singing, drumming, and dancing for us. As interesting as this was, it was also very sad for me. Hearing these people make joyful noises to a false god broke my heart. The entire time I was praying that one day they would sing to the Lord Jesus Christ.

It won't be just the false religions that shock you. Poverty, odors, climate, hostility, language challenges, ethnic food, and lack of modern conveniences will hit you square between the eyes. Sometimes your response to the situation will not be what you expected. We usually find out a lot about ourselves when put in an unfamiliar environment.

Katie from the University of Mary Hardin-Baylor had this to say about her first weekend in Kenya:

It was neat walking around an African market, learning the culture, and just watching, but I thought that there would be no way I could ever live there. However, the first weekend there, I absolutely fell in love with Kenya. I felt at home.

Nothing can really prepare you to experience another culture. But you can remember this exhortation found in Colossians 4:2: "Devote yourselves to prayer, keeping alert in it with an attitude of thanksgiving" (NASB). Praying and being thankful go a long way in a new cultural setting. You will be more flexible if you have an attitude of thanksgiving. Remember, you can do all things through Christ who strengthens you. And you might even have fun if you choose to!

APPLY IT

1. What do you think would be the hardest cultural differences to face? Scripturally, what should you do to maintain a godly attitude?

2. Read Acts 17:16–34. What was Paul's technique for cross-cultural experiences?

3. What did you learn from the two students about facing new cultures?

For further study (optional):
Maintaining a joyful attitude is good advice for anyone experiencing a new culture. Read Philippians 3 and 4 and make a list of what Paul has to say about joy.

WILLING to BEND

Flexibility is all about keeping a good attitude at a moment's notice. As the saying goes, "Shine, don't whine." Life is full of surprises, but if you can keep a good attitude and remain fluid, you will be better prepared for student missions. You will have a very unusual mission experience if everything goes smoothly.

This week, you've learned about being content in all circumstances, and you've been given examples of how world cultures vary through several student stories. It would be arrogant to think that your culture is better than other cultures. That's why we have to meet people where they are. Remember that Paul said, "To the weak I became weak, that I might win the weak. I have become all things to all men, that I may by all means save some" (1 Cor. 9:22, NASB).

How do you become all things to all men so that some may be saved? It's simple: listen and observe. If you listen to God, to your field contact, to the people group you visit, and to things you have learned in this book—and, on top of that, you observe the people group to see what works and what doesn't work while you are on the field—*then* you will have a good idea of how to reach the lost. Being willing to bend in order to find a way to reach the lost will mature you spiritually and develop your character. This willingness on your part will teach you to utterly depend on God and to rely on His strength.

Tony, a student from the University of North Florida in Jacksonville, thought he had everything under control until his plans drastically changed and he had to come to a point of weakness.

After a week of planning, training, and rehearsing in Kentucky, we were ready. We had our portfolio of popular American music and a plan to rock out the Thai people and tell them about Jesus.

Then it was time for our first concert in front of 2,500 teenagers. We were the second band to perform. All we could think was, "Oh no, we have to follow that?!" The lead guitar player was ripping solos behind his head. The crowd loved them. We were nothing in comparison. These students were excited about an American rock band performing until they saw that the band only consisted of a keyboard player, an acoustic guitarist, and a drummer. In my eyes, the concert was a disaster. The audience did not know any of the songs we played, so they just looked at us with blank faces. If we wanted to make a connection, we would have to learn Thai rock music, a task that was almost impossible.

That's when God introduced us to Toy, an extraordinary guitarist, singer, and new Thai Christian! Toy taught us the most popular rock songs in Thailand. He quickly learned our songs, and off we went with a new look and sound. The crowds went crazy because they loved the songs we played. During the concert, Toy shared his testimony of how Jesus saved him. We were able to demonstrate that Jesus loves all people.

Tony was willing to be flexible. He observed what the Thai students needed, and he was willing to listen to God's game plan. As a result, God provided a national to partner with them in order to reach the target group with the gospel. And Tony was very quick to give the credit to God.

Another student, Melanie from Winthrop University, had to be flexible while in the Philippines.

During my time in Manila for two months ministering to

university students, I fell so many steps backward. I wondered why students weren't responding well. I lowered to my knees more than ever before. That was about the time His Spirit started to move mightily on campus.

Through prayer and being open to change, God's Spirit was able to move. As you are walking in the Spirit, you will hear God and know the plans He has for you. He waits patiently while you fail time and time again in your own strength, but He would prefer for you to listen to Him from the beginning. In Jeremiah 29:11, God says, "For I know the plans that I have for you ... plans for welfare and not for calamity, to give you a future and a hope" (NASB). If you call on God and are open to His plans, He will direct you in the right way. Be flexible so that He can mold you.

Paul knew what it meant to face things that he didn't particularly want to confront, but he had a great attitude. "But we also rejoice in our sufferings, because we know that suffering produces perseverance; perseverance, character; and character, hope. And hope does not disappoint us, because God has poured out his love into our hearts by the Holy Spirit, whom he has given us" (Rom. 5:3–5).

Accountability to others will help you to remain flexible and to have a godly attitude like Paul. Perhaps your student mission team is a good place to start. Find three or four people of the same gender who will commit to meeting together on a weekly basis for 30 minutes. Pray for one another and for an unreached people group, and share what God is teaching you. Stay focused on the things that will help you become more Christlike and on mission each day. You'll be surprised at the difference this effort will make in your life.

APPLY IT

1. Look up these verses on what God has to say about plans: Psalm 48:14; Proverbs 3:6; Isaiah 42:16. Summarize what you learned.

2. How flexible are you? What do you think you need to do to be open to a change of plans?

3. If you are not already in an accountability group, form one or join one as soon as possible. List those you will ask to join you.

For further study (optional):
Think of a situation in which you chose not to be flexible to God's leadership. What happened as a result? In hindsight, what would you have done differently?

A CHANGE OF PLANS

Ben, a student at Wright State University, understands the reality of how plans change while serving in missions.

I was simply attending an on-campus worship service when out of nowhere came a call from somewhere deep inside me saying that I should go to India. I had heard that our campus ministry was arranging a team to go for the summer but brushed it off as something that wasn't for me. Little did I know that going on this trip would change my life.

I originally signed up to be on a medically experienced team to serve in a hospital, but after some plans were changed, I ended up on a team that would serve in schools in the slums of a major city. I simply had to accept what God was doing and go with the flow, because as the people there say, "Sub chalega," meaning "anything will work." When we landed in South Asia, it was 98 degrees at 11 p.m. I knew that this was going to be a completely new experience.

Although life was very different, it was great to immerse ourselves in the culture while we lived with national families. We even slept on the roof for four nights. In hindsight, I honestly feel as though I was the one benefiting. I learned more about my faith by sharing it with others and seeing how Christian workers serve. I thank God every day for the amazing opportunity and greatly look forward to the unending possibilities of the future.

By making the best of an unexpected situation, Ben learned about his own faith and looked forward to more opportunities in missions.

We can learn a lot from the apostle Paul and his many experiences of changed plans. In Acts 16, Paul and his team were passing through Phrygia and Galatia, but the Holy Spirit would not let them speak about Christ there. They listened. Then they tried to go to Bithynia, but the Spirit of Jesus would not let them go there. Finally, they came to Troas, and Paul received clear direction from a vision in which a man said, "Come over to Macedonia and help us."

Immediately, Paul and his team began their journey to Philippi, Macedonia. They didn't know exactly what they were supposed to do, but they looked for a place to pray. That's where they met Lydia and a group of women. They shared with the women, and Lydia became a Christian, along with her family members.

The story doesn't end there, because unexpected events kept coming their way. Lydia invited Paul and the team to stay at her house. Then, as they were walking again to the place of prayer, a young girl who was a fortune-teller followed them, shouting at Paul. He cast an evil spirit out of her, which led to his team being beaten by a crowd and thrown into jail. During the night, there was an earthquake and their chains were broken. This event led to the jailer's repentance, and his entire family came to Christ. Paul and his team were then released by the officials.

This amazing chain of events happened because Paul listened to the Spirit to know what to do. Listening to God's Spirit often brings about action that you might not expect. Proverbs 16:9 says, "The mind of man plans his way, but the LORD directs his steps" (NASB). You might have a plan for your future career, spouse, or home. You may even have a plan concerning your participation in world missions. The thing you should remember is that the Lord will direct your steps if you will listen to Him. If you go on a mission trip, remember to be open to His guidance and realize that changes in plans more than likely will occur.

Aryn from Texas A&M University describes how she had to be flexible while on a student mission trip to Mexico.

A village we went to wasn't on our agenda. The pastor for the intended village never showed up, so our national partner found another pastor. That morning, the pastor had bought a plot of land in a village that had no church and he was considering how to start evangelizing. That night we were able to be a part of the first evangelism contact in that village. The pastor got to meet the people, and the people were able to hear about the love of Christ. The pastor now has a list of contacts to visit because about a dozen people accepted Christ that night.

While in East Asia, Austin from Hardin Simmons University also had to be flexible.

We returned from a five-day journey in which our task was to conduct free medical clinics in small rural villages. The original plan was to conduct clinics for two days in each village, but because of a slight miscommunication, we were only able to stay three days total. We spent our nights in a medium-sized city and then drove a few hours in the mornings to small towns. We had brought a supply of medicine, which was enough to sustain a small army. This made hauling it everywhere a pain in the neck. But hey, who cares, right?

Sometimes you just have to keep a sense of humor when plans change. Otherwise, you'll get frustrated. God has a way of giving you many opportunities to smile while serving as a student missionary. Take life as it comes—laugh and enjoy the ride!

APPLY IT

1. Read Acts 16:6–40. Even the apostle Paul got frustrated at times. How did he make the best of constantly changing plans?

2. Write out and memorize Isaiah 30:21.

3. How can a sense of humor help you when plans are changed?

For further study (optional):
Go to an online Bible site and do a word search on "plans." See which verses speak to you concerning the difference between man's plans and God's plans.

BEING A SERVANT

"For though I am free from all men, I have made myself a slave to all, that I might win the more" (1 Cor. 9:19, NASB). In this one statement, Paul gives the secret of how to bring others to faith in Jesus Christ. It's simple—be a servant.

If you want God to use you as a student missionary, then you have to give up all rights to comfort, plans, honor, convenience, and warm showers. Your attitude must be one of humility and willingness to serve others, even if it means digging pit toilets or caring for the destitute. What family you came from, where you live, how much money you have, or what school you attend mean nothing to those you will serve. If you think you are better than the people you are ministering to overseas, they will sense your pride. However, love and kindness, even when you are stuck with the lowliest of jobs, will speak loud and clear.

Julie from Houston Baptist University and her team saw an opportunity to serve and took it.

> One morning in South Asia, we were walking through the rice paddies and some women were out planting rice. They motioned for us to come to them and they invited us to work. So we plunged into shin-deep, muddy water and planted rice. It was so amazing! They typically sing while they work, so they asked us to sing. We sang a praise song while we worked with them. I could have spent the rest of my time in that village working.

In the name of Jesus, Julie and her team helped others, not worrying about the difficult work or muddy clothes. As a student missionary, you too will have the chance to work hard and serve others. Scripture emphasizes servant action. First Corinthians 10:24 says, "Let no one seek his own good, but that of his neighbor" (NASB). Putting others first is a good lesson in flexibility and compassion.

Kara from Augusta State University found out what being a servant was about when she volunteered to help out in two areas in Thailand hit by the devastating tsunami.

The Lord called me to help tsunami victims over my spring break. I wasn't ready to leave Thailand when the time came and prayed that some way, somehow, God would send me back. Then about two months later, He opened the door for me to return to help rebuild a school that had been damaged.

Those three weeks were the best days of my life, even though they were also the most demanding. There's no greater feeling than knowing that you are shining the light of Jesus. I have found that "my life is worth nothing unless I use it for doing the work assigned me by the Lord Jesus—the work of telling others the Good News about God's wonderful kindness and love" (Acts 20:24, NLT). I helped to build houses, distribute food and water, love on the people, clean up debris, rebuild a school, and share Jesus with them.

Out of this terrible disaster, God's love arose from devastation. I've come to the point where I'm willing to lay my life down for Christ. He died and suffered for me, so I'm willing to do the same for Him.

Kara was a servant to desperate people, and through her servanthood she laid down her life for Jesus and His purposes for her.

Jesus, the King of kings, is the epitome of humility. Scripture tells us that "although He existed in the form of God, [Christ Jesus] did not regard equality with God a thing to be grasped, but emptied Himself, taking the form of a bond-servant, and being made in the likeness of men. And being found in appearance as a man, He humbled Himself by becoming obedient to the point of death, even death on a cross" (Phil. 2:6–8, NASB).

Are you willing to allow God to use you however He sees fit? Are you willing to be a servant to others and to follow the examples of Paul, Peter, and even Jesus?

A student from Boston University, Cristina, discovered a new motto for her life when she went to South Asia.

During one of our prayerwalks, I spotted what is now my favorite trash can. Stenciled on the front in white letters were the words USE ME. How appropriate. That trash-can slogan became my prayer for the rest of the trip. Letting go of all the preconceived plans I had when I stepped off the plane, I asked God to use me in any way He saw fit. Only then was I able to see India as He truly saw it. India has one-fifth of the world's population, and less than 3 percent know the Lord. If we do not show them God's love, who will?

Being a flexible servant will go a long way in experiencing a successful mission. Let your life's motto be "Lord, use me."

APPLY IT

1. What do you think it means to be a servant? Support with Scripture.

2. Reflecting on your life, how can you be a better servant to others?

3. Read Matthew 19:29–30. What do you think Jesus meant by these words?

For further study (optional):
Read Ephesians 6:5–8. Make a list of the instructions given to slaves. How can you apply this list to your life?

TELL THE STORY

Everyone loves a story. When a teacher or pastor uses an illustration to explain something, it's much easier to remember the lesson.

Jesus was a master at storytelling. You can read the four Gospels and find deep spiritual truths explained through stories such as the prodigal son and the lost sheep. Not only is the Bible full of parables that make specific points, but it is also a historical record of the lives of real people like David, Ruth, Job, Daniel, Samuel, and hundreds more. These ordinary people followed God the best way they knew how, and reading their stories in Scripture gives us instruction, inspiration, and sometimes even humor.

Every follower of Christ has a story to tell. Although for the most part we can't wait to tell our friends funny or exciting news, the thought of sharing the gospel and our own spiritual testimony can make us break into a cold sweat. In a world absorbed with being politically correct, we hesitate to share the good news of Jesus because we don't want to offend anyone. The devil is having a good laugh over his successful scheme of instituted political correctness in all areas of our lives, even our spiritual lives.

If we truly understood how many unreached people around the world are plunging into darkness, our discomfort of sharing the gospel would seem insignificant. Amanda from the University of Texas at Arlington said,

In Japan, I visited a university's English class. One girl offered me some hard candy in the shape of Buddha, saying, "Eat it. It will make you happy!" I asked her by what power it causes someone to be happy. She had no answer. I rephrased it, "Where does the Buddha's power come from?" Another girl said, "From heaven!" I inquired, "Well, what's in heaven?" After another long pause, she replied, "I think there are many flowers." The candy giver added, "And there is only happiness and no guilt or sadness." I then asked how she knew these things. "I heard a story once about a man who went to heaven and saw these things—that it was good and happy and there was no guilt—and he came back and said everyone should go there. So we will all go there someday."

If someone had said this about eternity to you, maybe you wouldn't have known how to respond. When dealing with any unbeliever, it's best to lovingly share the truth of the Word. "Always be prepared to give an answer to everyone who asks you to give the reason for the hope that you have. But do this with gentleness and respect" (1 Peter 3:15). This Buddha candy story is just one example of how people across the world need to hear the truth of the Word of God. You will learn more about sharing Scripture on day 3.

So how can we get past the fear of sharing the greatest story on earth? This week of lessons will help you develop a strategy for sharing the gospel as you personally deal in prayer with any inhibitions you have about sharing your faith.

Although missions can certainly begin in your own neighborhood or country, you may need to look beyond your nation's borders when considering the lost people of the world. As Jimmy from Rice University said,

> I thought it would be more cost effective to convert everyone in my own town first before venturing elsewhere. At least this is what I believed before I went to East Asia. But the Lord blessed my summer there and gave me a vision of devoting my life to a mission field that is not necessarily in my backyard.

YOUR **PERSONAL STORY**

Think back to the time when you became a Christian. Whether you were a young child or a teenager, you should remember most of what happened and where it happened. Perhaps a parent, family member, Sunday School teacher, friend, or pastor led you to the Lord. Maybe you started reading the Bible for yourself and you believed the words of Jesus. Whatever circumstances led to you believing in Jesus Christ and allowing Him to control your life, you have a story to tell.

A testimony is a true, firsthand account of an event given by a witness. The apostle Paul shares his testimony in Acts 22:1–21 and Acts 26:1–23. He told his story in the language of the crowd in Acts 22, beginning with a brief account of his pre-Christian life of being a devout Jew and persecutor of Christians. Next, Paul tells of his Damascus road experience when Jesus Himself spoke to him from heaven, asking Paul why he was persecuting Him. Paul was blinded, a man named Ananias came to him under the instruction of the Lord, and Paul was given a commission to be a witness to the Gentiles. Then Paul was baptized.

Your personal testimony needs to be brief, especially when sharing in a culture that is different from your own. You shouldn't concentrate on details or clichés that could only be understood in your own culture. You shouldn't use "church" words such as "sanctified", "justified", "accepting" Jesus into your heart, and "salvation". These terms and phrases cannot be translated in most languages.

Because this book is not a study on individual cultures of the world, you may want to have your mission trip supervisor contact the missionary you'll work with so that he or she can direct you in writing the story of your personal salvation experience. That way, your story can be better translated into the language of the people group.

Danah, a high school student in Ohio, discovered the power of sharing her personal story while on a mission trip to Ecuador.

Once we arrived in Ecuador, we were able to talk at many different schools. I was nervous at first because of the language barrier, but in the end everything worked out even better than expected. When I told my testimony, some of the kids were going through exactly what I went through.

A basic way to organize a brief testimony of no more than three minutes is to follow this pattern:

- What was your life like before you received Christ?

- How did you meet Jesus? What experiences, Bible verses, and/ or persons helped you realize your need for Christ?

- How did you invite Christ into your life?

- What immediate changes took place in you when you believed in Jesus and gave Him control of your life?

- Since that time, what difference has Christ made in your life?

- What does Jesus' presence mean in your daily life?

If you are sharing your personal salvation story through a translator on the mission field, if possible you should go over the story with your translator first so that you can work out any problems of understanding.

Even before arriving on the field, practicing what it will be like to work with a translator is a good idea, too. Ask a friend to act as your "translator" and repeat what you say after every sentence or two. With this practice, you'll have a true idea of how long your testimony will be when given through a translator and also how to keep your train of thought going when it is broken up into phrases and sentences. Your friend can also help you reword cultural clichés.

Later this week, you will learn that sharing your personal salvation story is only part of sharing Christ with another person. The most important part of sharing the gospel is sharing words from the Bible. The Bible translates much better than your story, so keep in mind that your personal story will help support what the Bible says, not the other way around.

Let's look at what three students had to say about sharing their personal stories overseas. Ben from Berea College said,

> During my service in Poland, my team and others ran an English camp in the city of Sopot. We decided that everyone was going to give a testimony during evening worship. I was worried about what I was going to say. Growing up in a family that went to church faithfully was not too common in Poland. I prayed about it, and the night before I gave my testimony, God revealed to me what I should say.
>
> I read the story of the woman at the well and realized that all people's relationships with Christ develop the same way as her relationship. Jesus approached me even though I was not worthy. He revealed to me that I was a sinner and that I needed the true life only He offers. And when I believed, I wanted

others to experience the true life that Jesus gave to me. I told the youth at that camp that the reason I had come to their country was to share what Jesus has done for me. And if God touched their hearts as much as He touched mine while I made that last statement, I am sure God spoke to them.

Notice that God revealed to Ben that he should share a story out of the Bible, a story that the people could relate to easier than Ben's personal testimony.

Another student, Brice from Dallas Baptist University, used personal examples to connect with an audience. He had this to say about sharing in Japan:

God used me to share my story with some ladies attending a Bible study. None are Christians yet, but they are seeking. I was able to tell them about my own struggles and me trying to control my life. They could relate to what I was saying. And they were so excited because God had brought me out of that lifestyle and that gave them hope.

Carrie from the University of the Cumberlands was able to share her testimony and see a young girl become a Christian as a result.

A Muslim named Elmira was studying in France. She came to our Bible study and began a conversation with me. I soon found out that Elmira was not a Christian. I prayed that someone would share with her the love of Jesus Christ. Little did I know that it would be me! One night during church, Elmira walked in late. I turned around to see her beautiful face, and God showed me her lost soul. So I got ready! After finding out that Elmira was leaving to go to her home country, I fought my way through the crowd after the service. I was too late. She was gone.

However, I learned she would be at our Bible study on Tuesday. I was confident that Elmira would be saved that night. But Elmira never came. Crushed and confused, I questioned what God had shown me.

God is faithful, though. On Sunday, I saw Elmira walk into church once again. This time, my walk to Elmira after church was even quicker. I was nervous, but I trusted God. Before I sat down beside her, Elmira began talking about God. I shared with her my testimony and the sacrifice that Jesus had made for us. That night, Elmira's life was changed. She asked Jesus Christ to forgive her of her sins and to come live in her life "Toujours" (always).

Sharing your testimony is scary, exhilarating, and life changing. It's part of taking a risk for God. Being prepared helps a lot with the initial fear. As you depend upon God and ask Him what He would have you say, He will give you the right words and time to share!

APPLY IT

1. What are some common elements that you noticed in the three student stories?

2. Read Acts 26:1–29. Make an outline or list of Paul's testimony before King Agrippa. How do you think King Agrippa was affected by Paul's story?

3. Write your personal testimony, following the bullets in this lesson. Practice reading it aloud and time it to see if it is less than three minutes long.

For further study (optional):
Read Acts 5:17–42, and write down why the apostles would not stop telling the good news.

LIFESTYLE EVANGELISM

How many hypocrites do you know? Chances are that you know at least one. But before you start making a list of all the frauds you know, remember that only Jesus was perfect.

Jesus, the sinless Son of God, got really ticked off with hypocrites. He said, "Woe to you, teachers of the law and Pharisees, you hypocrites! You shut the kingdom of heaven in men's faces. You yourselves do not enter, nor will you let those enter who are trying to. ... You travel over land and sea to win a single convert, and when he becomes one, you make him twice as much a son of hell as you are" (Matt. 23:13, 15). Ouch!

Jesus also cautioned people about hypocrisy in his famous Sermon on the Mount.

> Do not judge, or you too will be judged. For in the same way you judge others, you will be judged, and with the measure you use, it will be measured to you. Why do you look at the speck of sawdust in your brother's eye and pay no attention to the plank in your own eye? How can you say to your brother, 'Let me take the speck out of your eye,' when all the time there is a plank in your own eye? You hypocrite, first take the plank out of your own eye, and then you will see clearly to remove the speck from your brother's eye. (Matt. 7:1-5)

The reality is that we all sin, even Christians. Jesus lovingly accepts us as we are and tells us to go and leave our lives of sin (John 8:11). If you remember the story of the woman who committed adultery and was about to be stoned, Jesus quietly told the crowd that the person who had never sinned should throw the first stone (John 8:3–11). That shut everyone up, because they knew they all were sinners.

Even though we might have messed up in our past, we each have a choice about who we are going to be in Christ today and in the future, and whether we will be a positive witness for Jesus or a negative one. People who don't know the Word of God or Jesus will look at Christians to see how they act.

The apostle Peter often made mistakes and even denied Christ, but he learned from his faults and became a great leader in the early church. David, who was beloved by God, had an adulterous affair and arranged for the murder of his mistress's husband. The Bible is not filled with perfect people but with those who knew God and repented.

People are searching for truth today. They are looking for something to believe in, something that is real. As believers, we are to accurately represent Jesus. To do that, we must rely on Him, walk with Him, spend time in the Word, and pray. You may never fully realize what impact you have on others by demonstrating a Christian life.

Several students who were short-term missionaries overseas got a glimpse of how others watch them. Monica from Florida State University said,

Sitting at the university campus overlooking the Panama Canal, I was asked, "What's so different about you? Why are you not like us? Why don't you do the things we do?" Once again, as I had done for 10 weeks, I did my best to explain that the difference was the power of God living in me. In the melting pot of culture, language, ideas, and religions that makes up the country of Panama, these students have the daunting task of finding truth. I told my friends that God desires a personal relationship with them. I told of salvation that comes through faith alone and not through works. I told of the God who calls us to follow in His footsteps.

Another student, Derek from Brazosport College, was emotional when he realized how God was using his team in Eastern Europe.

During the day, we played with the village kids at camp. Many seeds were planted for the kingdom. As our adviser came to pick us up at the end of the day, a gentleman stopped him on the way up the mountain. He told him, "Thank you for bringing those students up here to play with our kids. You can tell that those boys really care about our children. There is something different about those boys." Once I heard that, I was moved to tears. It showed that He is moving through us even when we don't see it.

Kinsey from the University of North Florida said,

While in Ghana, I had the opportunity to be a "mom" to a newborn baby girl for two weeks. Her mother died, and I offered to care for her at the hospital with the love of Christ. While caring for this baby, a Muslim nurse watched me. She told me that she wanted to be a Christian because she could see Christ's love in me. I had the honor of walking her through accepting Christ.

Jon from Dallas Baptist University learned about being an ambassador for Christ. He said,

In Germany, our team performed a drama. I played the part of Jesus in the skit because of my long hair and facial hair. After we finished the skit, a little boy looked me straight in the eyes and asked, "Jesus?" It really hit me that this boy thought that

I was Jesus. It was a powerful reminder to me that we are supposed to represent Jesus to others.

From these student stories, it is evident that people do indeed watch us. In a final story, Sarah, a student in Oklahoma, had this to say:

On December 26, 2004, the doors of several countries were flung open by the tsunami. Seven months later we walked through those doors into the arms of those still trying to wake up from the nightmare. We painted, cleaned up trash and sewage, and smiled. We arrived being unsure of what we were going to do or even how to wear our head coverings _ but God held our hands as we held the hands of those we worked alongside and met with each day.

We taught each other words from our languages and had discussions about life. We laughed and cried with them. We introduced them to ultimate Frisbee. And on our last night, two students came to a person at our house and said, "Where are your students? We need to talk to them! You see, we have religion, but they have faith. We want to know about this."

A worker was able to share the gospel with them that day. We suddenly realized that although we barely spoke a word of their language, they saw the hope that we have. Religion is tiresome and empty—faith is what they desire. They just needed someone to show them The Way.

Our actions speak loud and clear. God calls us to represent Christ to the nations and to those in our own neighborhoods and schools. Before you ever master an organized plan to share the gospel, make sure your life is a positive testimony of the love of Christ.

APPLY IT

1. Read John 4:7–39, the story of the woman at the well. Make a list of her actions throughout the passage. Summarize in a sentence or two what you think was her testimony of salvation. As a result of her encounter with Jesus, what did she do publicly?

2. Do you think that you really grasp how lost the world is without Jesus? Why or why not? How did the Buddha candy story in the introduction to this week demonstrate lostness?

3. Reflecting on the student stories, what did you learn about lifestyle evangelism? How can you apply what you learned to your life?

For further study (optional):
Joseph had many chances to demonstrate a godly life even in hardship and when false accusations were made against him. Read Genesis 39 and describe Joseph's lifestyle.

SHARING GOD'S WORD IN HIS TIMING

There are many ways that you will have the chance to share the gospel while serving on the mission field. We've looked at sharing your personal story and lifestyle evangelism. Being involved in chronological Bible storying (telling the main stories of the Bible from Genesis to the ascension of Christ), drama, and singing are other important methods. The most effective way to share the gospel is by sharing Bible stories in the language of the people.

More than likely, you will not know the language. That's OK. The missionary or national you will work with most likely will have evangelistic tools such as the *JESUS* film, New Testaments, and a translator. If you know the basic verses or stories in the Bible that can lead someone to Christ, then you will be prepared the best way possible.

Second Timothy 2:15 says, "Do your best to present yourself to God as one approved, a workman who does not need to be ashamed and who correctly handles the word of truth." You need to know how to lead someone to Christ through the Word alone. The Word speaks to any people group when your personal story cannot. That's why you don't need to be timid about sharing God's Word. Your story probably won't convict anyone of sin, but God's Word does. "For the word of God is living and active. Sharper than any double-edged sword, it penetrates even to dividing soul and spirit, joints and marrow; it judges the thoughts and attitudes of the heart" (Heb. 4:12).

When in a foreign culture, it is better to stick with Bible verses instead of illustrations used in a tract or witnessing program (unless you are using verses with a tool such as the Evangecube.) Here are some verses and statements that you should memorize:

- *People avoid God and rebel against Him.*
"For all have sinned and fall short of the glory of God" (Rom. 3:23).

- *Yet God loves you and wants to free you from sin, to offer you a new life of hope.*
"But God demonstrates his own love for us in this: While we were still sinners, Christ died for us" (Rom. 5:8).

- *To give you this life of hope, God made a way through His Son, Jesus Christ.*
"For the wages of sin is death, but the gift of God is eternal life in Christ Jesus our Lord" (Rom. 6:23).

- *Faith in Christ is a personal decision.*
"That if you confess with your mouth, 'Jesus is Lord,' and believe in your heart that God raised him from the dead, you will be saved. For it is with your heart that you believe and are justified, and it is with your mouth that you confess and are saved" (Rom. 10:9–10).

- *You can become a Christian now.*
"For, 'Everyone who calls on the name of the Lord will be saved'" (Rom. 10:13).

Other verses to memorize or mark in your Bible include John 3:16–18; John 10:9–11; John 10:27–30; John 11:25; John 14:6; John 17:3; Acts 4:12; 1 John 5:11–13; and Revelation 3:20.

When you are serving in a more restrictive area and/or where many people cannot read, telling Bible stories is more successful than sharing a list of verses. People can remember stories, and they will repeat them.

The stories of what man did to separate himself from God (Gen. 3) and what God did to bring us back to Him (the story of Jesus) are good places to start. Two other stories to memorize are the woman at the well (John 4:7–39) and when Paul and Silas were in jail (Acts 16:16–33).

After you have shared from the Bible, do not immediately press someone to pray for salvation unless the person is overwhelmingly responsive and wants to repent at that moment. This is not about you racking up numbers of converts to report to your church at home. Your mission supervisor and you should be clued in to how the culture works concerning conversion. For instance, it is very common to ask a group of Africans if they want to become Christians after seeing an evangelistic film or hearing an evangelistic sermon. Many in the crowd will raise their hands to accept Christ, but very few will actually convert. They raise their hands because it would be rude to the visitors not to do as they ask.

"Don't pick green fruit" is a statement to remember in these situations. God's timing is perfect. Most likely, you may only be a seed planter when you share the gospel in an international setting. Besides, the cost is great to convert to Christianity, sometimes bringing intense persecution. The person needs to have time to count the cost so that he will truly convert. God will send other missionaries or Christian nationals to lead people to salvation in God's timing. You may have the privilege of seeing the fruit of your labor while you're on the field, but when you're serving on a short-term mission project, it's not guaranteed. Be sensitive to the Holy Spirit and to the training of the missionary who lives in the area you go to serve.

Philip got a message from God and was told to go down a desert road. It was on this road that Philip ran into an Ethiopian who was ready to hear the gospel. He invited Philip to explain God's Word to him. Philip guided this man to Jesus, and the man believed. God's Spirit had prepared the way. Philip's availability to share the good news in God's timing gave him the privilege to be involved (Acts 8:26–39).

If a person does want to become a Christian, then consider these things: be sure you are discerning the Holy Spirit's leading, be clear in what you are asking the person to do, know that you can speak the Word of God with authority, and avoid getting into arguments or chasing rabbits. You may choose to share the gospel ABCs:

- *Admit* that you are a sinner and repent (Rom. 3:23; Acts 3:19).

- *Believe* that Jesus Christ died and rose again so that your sins could be forgiven and you could be made right with God (Rom. 6:23; 5:8).

- *Confess* that you want Jesus to be the leader of your life (Rom. 10:9–10).

In the next lesson, you will see these principles in action as you read firsthand accounts of students who shared their faith on the mission field.

APPLY IT

1. On note cards, write these verses: John 3:16–18; John 10:9–11; John 10:27–30; John 11:25; John 14:6; John 17:3; Acts 4:12; Romans 3:23; Romans 5:8; Romans 6:23; Romans 10:9–10; Romans 10:13; 1 John 5:11–13; and Revelation 3:20. Memorize these verses over the next month.

2. Practice repeating the gospel ABCs and retelling the stories found in John 4:7–39 and Acts 16:16–33.

3. Read Acts 8:26–39. Why is it important to be sensitive to God's timing when sharing your faith or inviting someone to become a Christian?

4. Read 1 Corinthians 3:5–8. Who is the one who causes the growth—the true conversion that is lived out?

For further study (optional):
Think of an example of a quick conversion in the Bible and an example of a slower consideration. Compare the two. If you can't think of examples, you might compare these two passages: John 4:46–53 and John 3:1–21.

MAKING THE MOST OF OPPORTUNITIES

"Be very careful, then, how you live—not as unwise but as wise, making the most of every opportunity, because the days are evil" (Eph. 5:15–16).

Opportunities for God to use you are around every corner. Being an encourager, a servant, a witness, or a friend are just a few of the ways He uses Christians every day. Because of our busyness, we are not always aware of opportunities that God provides for us to share the gospel with someone. Colossians 4:2 tells us how we can discern these opportunities: "Devote yourselves to prayer, being watchful and thankful." As you walk with God in a prayerful attitude, you will become more aware of what He wants you to do each day.

Today's lesson will allow you to see how God used students as they made themselves available to Him. So sit back and enjoy the stories!

Erica from Anderson College was nervous about sharing the gospel at first.

Upon my arrival to Manila, I found myself in culture shock. Not only was this my first overseas mission trip, but I was required to daily witness to students on the college campus. I have never been outgoing about my faith. I wanted to pack up and go home. I reminded God that I was traveling 2,000 miles to teach, not to witness!

For a few days, I simply refused to believe that I was going to witness. Later that week, what did we do? Go out witnessing. Being stubborn, I sat on a wall even though I felt that the Lord wanted me to talk to a group of people. I tried to ignore God, but it didn't work. I believe that God literally kicked me, for I jumped off the wall and walked to the group. As I shared and asked them questions, it was not that bad.

As the weeks progressed, I was still nervous about witnessing, but I felt the peace of God. Each time I prayed for words to say, I would find them when I needed them. Exodus 4:12 says, "Now therefore, go, and I will be with your mouth and teach you what you shall say (NLT)." The greatest blessing came when I got to see changes in various students who found the joy of knowing Christ.

Cassi from Tarrant County College shared how God spoke through her while sharing her faith.

After initially talking to a Muslim man and his family, another opportunity arose to visit them in their home. We got deep into conversation and the Word for hours. Toward the end of our conversation, the man's head was buried in his handkerchief. He was weeping. God had spoken to him, and he truly wanted to repent. We said that God would forgive and love him as His own. His wife and sister-in-law began to weep, for they knew they had been misled by the teachings of Islam. They surrendered their lives completely to God. It was not anything any of us said. It was what God said through us.

Kristi from the University of Miami took the opportunity to share with a Buddhist.

I was in a village about a five-days walk from Mount Everest base camp. In the mornings, I would go downstairs to the dining room area of the lodge and have time with Jesus. A worker at the lodge would ask questions about God, Christianity, and my beliefs. One morning, we were talking about meditation. I showed him Psalm 145 and gave him my Bible to use for the day. That evening we sat down to discuss the psalm. He had translated the entire psalm into his language! Along with a translator, we spent the next several hours discussing different aspects of Christianity. Although he did not become a Christian that evening, he did request a Bible in his own language.

I gave him an English Bible. Every day he would be tucked away in a corner reading the Bible with two dictionaries to assist in his understandings. I know that God will call him to His kingdom soon enough. It is a miracle this Buddhist is willing to seek God's face.

Playing basketball gave Chad from Texas Wesleyan University an opportunity to share the gospel with Asian students.

In East Asia, I enjoyed going to a campus and playing basketball. Playing basketball allowed me to establish some relationships. One of the guys invited me to his dorm room to teach me the local lingo. This came at a very crucial time because I was really getting frustrated with the language barrier. Then I invited him and other people to our apartment, and we talked to them about the Bible and Jesus. They asked lots of questions. Afterward we gave them copies of the Bible in their language.

Tendai from the University of Syracuse had to wait patiently for God's timing to share the gospel with a Chinese teenager.

Iris is 17 years old. We go out to eat together, shop, and walk around the city. I speak to her of my Jesus, giving her a JESUS film and a Chinese Bible. She watches the film; she begins to read Luke. She is intrigued but hesitant. I ask her if she has any questions, but she needs more time to read and think. "Father, give me patience. I want so badly for her to believe!" I wait days, a week, two weeks. She is hearing more of God in my English class and asking questions. Then one day, I am sitting in the cafeteria. Iris shows up and asks me to go on a walk with her. She has a tract that I gave her earlier. I ask if she believes in Jesus. She says yes. I ask her if she would like to pray. She is now my sister in Christ.

Iris continues in the Word since her heart is on fire. She takes it home to her small village. Her grandparents are intrigued. I give her a Bible and tract to take them. She also shares with her roommate and gives her a tract. The Word is going forth. I stand in awe.

Rene from Rhodes College had a very unexpected opportunity to share the gospel during her trip to China.

As we climbed up one side of the stairs, a pair of Chinese friends climbed up the other side. My teammate smiled at them and said hi, and we continued to walk on. About five seconds later, we heard the sound of footsteps running toward us. The girls wanted to talk. As it turned out, they were from a university down the street, and they were English majors.

One of the girls asked me if I was a Christian. Responding with an excited, "Yes! I follow Jesus," I asked if she knew what that meant. She proceeded to tell me that her grandmother had been a Christian and that she had passed away last month. Her grandmother's dying wish was that her family would all become Christians, and her wish now was to one day be reunited with her grandmother in heaven. Our conversation eventually led to praying together in a stairwell where both of these girls received Christ.

God will use you, too, as you watch for opportunities to share the gospel!

APPLY IT

1. What do you think it means to make the most of the opportunities God gives you? Give an example of an opportunity to share the gospel that God gave you recently.

2. Underline key phrases in the student stories that show how these students made the most of an opportunity.

3. Read Acts 10:19–48. How did Peter make the most of this opportunity that came out of the blue?

For further study (optional):
Think of three people in Scripture who made the most of an opportunity to share the gospel. Explain what they did in each situation.

WITNESSING IN HOSTILE ENVIRONMENTS

A national church planter who has been involved in a Muslim country since early 2005 has seen nine Muslims come to Christ. He has faced quite a challenge—evangelizing in the face of certain persecution. He has been beaten and confronted by Muslim religious leaders. But he continues to risk all so that the message of Jesus Christ may go out into the Muslim community.

In another area, as a result of persecution, one Indian seeker has been afraid to meet with local believers to talk about Jesus. He became interested in knowing more about Christianity after Western Christian volunteers shared Jesus Christ with him. But a few locals have become very suspicious and antagonistic toward Christianity. As a result, it is unwise for an outsider to be seen talking with this seeker, since it would cause unnecessary pressure on him.

In numerous places around the world, people are persecuted for their faith in Jesus, or even for showing interest in Christianity. Christian workers in high-security areas have very good insight on the best ways to witness and disciple. If you are considering a mission project to an area where believers are persecuted, then it is of the utmost importance for you and your project supervisor to be sensitive to the training you receive before and during your experience.

If you are considering a mission trip to a high-security country, be sure to share with your family ahead of time that you are going to a hostile environment. Ask these questions prior to the mission experience: "Can I bring Bibles or Christian literature/movies into the country? Should I go by an alias? Can I mention the name of the missions organization with which I'm affiliated? Can I share my faith openly or only when I'm asked? Can I attend or organize a Christian meeting? Can I tell people back home where I'm going?"

Many of us in the Western world have no idea what being persecuted for our faith really means. When a man walked into a Christian hospital in Yemen in 2002 and murdered three American missionaries because his wife had been influenced by Christianity while being treated at the hospital, persecution for faith became a stark reality for the International Mission Board. Later, five Christian aid workers were shot in Iraq in 2004 because they were Westerners, and four died. In addition, countless nationals associated with missionaries have been murdered.

A Christian worker needs the freedom to continue working or to begin sharing in a country that students may visit for a short time. This cannot be stressed enough—be sensitive! Find out what you should and should not do from the missionary or national contact. As a worker from North Africa stated, "Let [persecution] be for who Jesus is and not for the outsider."

Before you think that you shouldn't go to certain places, remember that other students are serving in hostile environments. Scot described his experience serving in Afghanistan with college students.

The last day of our trip, two of my English students and their friend came to see me while I ate breakfast. I had made an appointment to see them earlier in the week, but they did not show. I thought they were coming to say a quick goodbye, but they had much more on their minds than that. The students jumped at the offer to come inside and drink tea. They began to share that since we had come into their small village, they had been thinking about their religion and my religion.

The students were of a people group the Taliban persecuted. Many people in the area fled to Iran. They had expected to be welcomed by their brothers of the same faith. When they arrived, they were treated badly. These events made them think that maybe Islam was not the way to heaven. So they came to ask more about Jesus. That morning, my teammates and I were able to share stories of the fall of man, Abraham, Moses and the Law, and finally, Jesus and hope. The students were captivated by the stories. They wanted a Bible to read these stories for themselves.

Notice how the Lord led the refugees to ask more about Christianity and for a Bible. Scot had tried to organize a meeting, but God brought the nationals to him instead. These students counted the cost and chose to approach the Christian to find out more about a faith of love.

God has a way of designing opportunities to reveal Himself in any region, and He is especially creative in hostile environments. Beth from Francis Marion University tells of her experience in South Asia.

In the Khumbu mountain region of Nepal, God moved phenomenally in the hearts of the people during my summer trip. My three partners and I had two porters who helped carry our bags to the villages that we planned to visit. The older Buddhist porter had been inquiring about Jesus. The awesome two-year worker with us gave him a Nepali Bible, and he was reading it almost every time we saw him. The younger Buddhist porter was also interested, so we gave him a Bible as well.

The two men were intrigued by this wonderful Man that they read of in the Bible, and they asked questions randomly and often. They observed the way that we acted toward each other.

Finally, after two weeks, they asked how to become a Christ follower. We were so excited that we had two new brothers in Christ! We began the discipling process with them. Everyone could see the love of the Lord in their faces. I do not know how their families accepted this new change in their lives, but I have prayed for them every day.

Prayer is essential in seeking the Father for chances to share. It's up to you to make the most of opportunities. Perhaps you will meet people at your school or in your community who come from countries that are hostile toward Christianity. You have much freedom in your own country to share Christ with internationals! But He may call you to go somewhere that people have few opportunities to hear the Word of God. See what He wants you to do. We will talk more about risk taking next week, so hang on!

APPLY IT

1. What do you know about persecution of Christians? How would you feel about the possibility of being severely persecuted for your faith?

2. Read Hebrews 11:1 to 12:3. Make a list of what these people of the Bible endured.

3. Read John 18:1 to 19:37. Think about the suffering Jesus endured. Write a prayer thanking Jesus for His great suffering on your behalf.

For further study (optional):
Do a Web search on persecution of Christians and research recent accounts.

WEEK 6

RISKY FAITH

"Tell me he's not going to do that," I said to my husband as we watched a missionary in his 20s put on a harness. He was preparing to plunge down the deep gorge over the Zambezi River at Victoria Falls, Zimbabwe. My husband watched with great enthusiasm while I held my breath. When I took a quick breath, I told my teenage son standing beside me not to get any ideas. He reassured me that he wouldn't bungee jump there until he was 18!

With one last smile to his audience on the bridge, the young man dove into the air and fell to the rushing water below, seemingly miles, and then jerked back up when the bungee rope stretched to its full length. Bouncing up and down several times, the ant-sized, exhilarated missionary deep in the gorge was finally pulled back to safety. I could breathe again. The crowd cheered, and he was ecstatic. He got the thrill of a lifetime.

Bungee jumping off of the Victoria Falls bridge is not a risk for God, but following Jesus is all about risk taking. In this final week of our study, you will examine what it means to take risks for God, read stories from students who took those risks, and learn about people in the Bible who risked everything for the Lord.

If you are going to be a student missionary, then you're taking a chance. You're risking your time, money, comfort, and even safety. More than that, you face the possibility of never being the same again. Your spiritual life won't be the same, and your view of the world will change. It's like taking a bungee jump—it's scary but thrilling.

Heather from the University of Montevallo took a risk and became a student missionary.

When I left for a mission trip to South Asia, I was interviewing for teaching jobs, but all that seemed to change once I went overseas. I've decided I want more out of life than mediocrity. I want to make an eternal impact. It isn't one specific thing in my life that's changed, but rather my outlook on life and God's calling on it. I learned the importance of international missions. Even on my first trip, I got to see how much can be accomplished in a few short days. People are ready to hear; they just need someone to tell them.

You've thought about many things since starting this book. Are you making a difference in the world through prayer? Is God calling you to serve as a student missionary? Do you trust God in everything? Are you flexible or frustrated? Are you sharing your story of what God means to you? And finally, are you willing to risk everything for God?

Heather wants to make an eternal impact. What about you?

By the way, the young man who bungee jumped returned to Africa a few years later as a career missionary with his new wife. They are risking everything for Jesus.

TAKE THE PLUNGE

If you feel called to go on a student mission trip, there comes a point in which you have to move beyond just considering student missions. Hopefully, your parents, friends, student ministry leader, and church know of your intentions; but signing the papers, getting a passport, raising support, and many other details have to start way in advance of a trip.

If you have no idea where to start, talk to your student ministry leader at church or school. This person may know of upcoming trips and can connect you with others interested in forming a team. You can also look online for student mission projects in many countries. Some great Web sites that provide information about student missions are www.thetask.org (International Mission Board), www.answerthecall.net (North American Mission Board), www.stemintl.org (Short-Term Evangelical Missions International), and www.shorttermmissions.com (represents over 70 Christian missions organizations).

You must apply for a passport about four months before your departure date. Many countries require visitors to have a visa, and you must have your passport before applying for a visa. If you are going with a team connected with a missions organization, you need to fill out all the necessary paperwork in advance. Inoculations may be required or recommended to enter certain countries, and sometimes these inoculations must be done six months prior to departure. Several months before your trip, you need to purchase plane tickets and consider appropriate packing guidelines. (For packing tips, see www.thetask.org.) You need to purchase health insurance to insure that you are adequately covered while traveling. And these are just a few of the logical details of a mission experience.

The challenge of raising financial support is a huge concern for students. When students find out how much money it costs to go on a mission trip, many say, "There's no way." Trusting God to provide is essential. "My God shall supply all your needs according to His riches in glory in Christ Jesus" (Phil. 4:19, NASB). You will find people who want to support you financially and prayerfully on a trip. Pray and ask God to show you which friends, neighbors, church members, and relatives should receive your support letter. (For sample support letters, see www.thetask.org/Students/Approved—funding.htm and click on "letters to prospective contributors.")

It is a blessing to watch God provide the financial support that you require. Many people who contribute to your trip can be compared to the Christians in Macedonia who begged to give toward the apostle Paul's missionary work, even though they didn't have much money (2 Cor. 8:1–5).

A high school student, Hunter, experienced this kind of giving. She said,

My father, younger sister, and I were led to be a part of a mission trip to Africa. At the time, my dad had just lost his job, and we knew that financially there was no way the three of us could go unless God intervened. We began to pray earnestly for God to provide.

God was tremendously faithful in His provisions. He impressed upon each of us to do all that we could and to trust Him to provide the rest. I can remember very vividly when my father came home and told my sister and me that a lady in our church had generously given $500 to both of us for our trip. She *said that God had not called her to go, but He had called her to help others go in her place. Members of our family and friends also helped to provide the means for us to go, but the generous gift from a lady that I barely knew really showed me God's faithfulness.*

God wants to teach you to accept His good gifts. He wants you to be able to worship Him as Jehovah Jireh, "The LORD Will Provide." In our culture, we want to be self-sufficient, but God wants us to depend on Him for all our needs. Being a student missionary will help you appreciate the generosity of others and the great provisions of your heavenly Father.

When you receive funds, keep a record of the support you receive, whether prayer or financial. Always thank each individual who prays for you and/or financially supports you. Then, when you return from your mission experience, update each of these individuals with a report of your trip. This helps them feel like they participated in a tangible way in your service to Christ.

APPLY IT

1. Read 2 Corinthians 8:1–5. How did the Macedonian Christians respond to Paul's missionary work?

2. Make a list of people you believe God wants you to invite to be on your support team.

3. Ask God to provide the financial and prayer support you need to be a student missionary. Pray for the people whom you will invite to support you.

For further study (optional):
In a Bible concordance, look up references to this name of God: Jehovah Jireh (Yehovah yireh)," The Lord Will Provide." Start with Genesis 22.

IS GOD'S WILL THE SAFEST PLACE?

How many times have you heard someone say, "The safest place to be is in the center of God's will"? Is this a statement that can be supported by Scripture? Think about it. How many people in the Bible had an easy life? In contrast, how many people in the Bible were martyred, beaten, or tortured? If you saw the movie *End of the Spear*, the five missionaries trying to reach the Waodoni of Ecuador absolutely believed that they were following God's will. Yet they were murdered by the people they tried to reach. For them and thousands of others before them, being in God's will was anything but *safe* by the world's definition.

If you are going to be a student missionary, there are precautions to keep you as safe as possible, but your safety cannot be guaranteed. Students have to weigh the very real risks they may face. In the 1990s, two students drowned during their mission assignment in Mexico. Others have been arrested for distributing Christian media. Additionally, your involvement with nationals can jeopardize their safety.

Ask yourself, "Am I willing to take these risks?" John the Baptist risked everything to prepare the way of the Lord. Eventually, he was beheaded (Matt. 14:1–12). Rahab put her life at risk to protect the spies sent by Joshua. In doing so, she found the one, true God (Josh. 2; 6:17, 25).

In 2005, a student team found themselves in an unexpected crisis. James from Johnson & Wales University shares a personal experience of the risk involved in student missions.

The mission was to penetrate a closed country in Southeast Asia with a DVD that presented the gospel. We were given some instructions about what to do if we were caught with DVDs in our backpacks. I ignored most of them, thinking no one would get arrested for preaching the gospel.

Our goal was to place our movie behind the store stock in video rental shops in hopes that it would later be found. We also placed the movie underneath layers of clothing in shops to be found after we left the country.

In our last and most anticipated city, we made a mistake. In our hurrying, we ran into the local police. They questioned us, held our passports, and found about 175 pieces of media in our bags. After a night of questioning, the officials asked us kindly to stay in the city until morning so that the chief could handle the matter. We politely rejected their offer and told them that we needed to be on our way. They kept us for another two hours and finally offered to escort us to another city. On the way, we stopped for gas, and the officials asked if we were hungry.

I started to wonder about their kindness. The only conclusion that I could come up with was that they must be taking us to a small, disclosed part of the wilderness to shoot and bury us. "They must know what was on those DVDs. Surely they know that we are missionaries and want to kill us", I thought. My leader and I sat in the back of that pickup truck, praying and quoting Scripture.

That night, I feared for my life. Previously, if you were to ask me if I would die for the gospel, I would give you a very enthusiastic yes. I would have never, until that night, known what that meant. The fear was real. Had I fulfilled all of God's purposes for me? Would I be able to leave the world I knew behind? God had more for me than this, didn't He? God let me dwell on my selfishness and soon interrupted with, **My passion is for My glory. My plans for you are perfect**. At ease, I knew that the gospel must be what I live and die for.

We were taken to an office of foreign affairs and placed in two small cells. Inside was a wastebasket filled with empty food containers, a large jug of water, a few bamboo mats, and more cockroaches than I had ever seen. They locked us in the cell with my guitar, our bags, and a small loaf of bread. We also had about 100 movies that were still concealed.

After spending the night, we were taken to the person in charge and waited for seven anxious hours. Camera flashes and shouting reporters greeted us. We were told to sit in front of the confiscated movies. They interrogated us, but our leader told us not to talk. She distinctly remembered the coordinator of the trip telling us that if we were caught, we shouldn't say anything to the press. The officials asked, "Why aren't you answering us? Don't you know that we have the power to set you free or to put you in jail? What you did was a serious crime in our country."

After a few hours, we were taken to the border and set free. Overjoyed, we sang praises. We had preached the Word and lived to tell about it.

James did not expect to be arrested for his faith. He thought that it wouldn't happen to him, so he ignored the safety precautions given by the trip coordinator. God allowed this situation to show James and his teammates the reality of what national Christians go through often and help them realize whether or not they were truly willing to die for the gospel.

A new worker in North Africa keeps the safety issue in perspective:

We have been praying about going to North Africa. So much is said regarding our safety and the safety of the people who may desire to receive Christ as their Savior. God has spoken clearly to me on the matter. We are so shortsighted sometimes. God's definition of "safety" is totally different from ours. We sometimes expect God to keep us safe. Safety to us can mean that we stay healthy and alive. It could mean that He keeps us safe from enemies in this world, danger, discomfort, or death. But safety to Him means salvation. That's it. Those who are saved are safe. If we are saved, then anything—ANYTHING—could happen and we would still be safe!

Do not be afraid. He has promised to be with us always. He has saved us! There is truly no reason to tell Him no. He has thought of everything . . . even possible "consequences" when He calls. His view of the consequences is that His perfect will is being accomplished. His ways are truly not our ways. "These things I have spoken to you, that in Me you may have peace. In the world you will have tribulation; but be of good cheer. I have overcome the world" (John 16:33, NKJV).

Listen to God's direction for your life. Nothing can happen to you unless it is filtered through God's fingers of love. When He shows you a risk to take, trust Him no matter what the outcome. In Joshua 1:9, God tells Joshua, "Be strong and courageous! Do not tremble or be dismayed for the LORD your God is with you wherever you go" (NASB).

APPLY IT

1. After reading James's story and the thoughts on safety by the worker in North Africa, what do you think about God's will and safety? What fears do you have about being a student missionary?

2. Read Matthew 14:1–12 and Joshua 2; 6:17, 25. Do you think that you have the courage of John the Baptist or Rahab? Why or why not?

3. Record your fears about being a student missionary. Ask God to make you strong and courageous, as He did Joshua.

For further study (optional):
Read Exodus 3:11–12; 4:1, 10–12. Moses had a good dose of the what-ifs when God asked him to take a risk. What was God's response to Moses' questions? How is God speaking to you through these verses?

WHEN THINGS GET WEIRD

As a student missionary, you are going to be personally challenged when you face unusual experiences. Expect it, because God wants to teach you something new. Hopefully, you won't have to experience a strange stomach illness. (Try to drink bottled drinks and eat cooked or packaged food.) However, you may encounter exotic foods that missionaries have reported eating, such as lizard eggs, rats on a stick, guinea pigs, donkey stew, or fried termites. After eating, you might have to use a toilet that consists of a hole in the ground, smells to high heaven, and has maggots crawling out of it. (I speak with experience!)

God has made you "adequate as servants of a new covenant" (2 Cor. 3:6, NASB), so remember that your adequacy to face challenges comes from God. Remember Philippians 4:13: "I can do all things through Him who strengthens me" (NASB).

Jennifer from Oklahoma spent the summer living in Andean villages where the gospel had never been shared.

The only familiar thing I had all summer was my backpack. Most of the other summer missionaries would probably agree that you experience God in a way that you never have before when you are forced to give up the things that you hold dear and that you think you need. I have come to an understanding of what it means to rely completely on God for everything, and I have realized my need for Him more and more every day.

In Acts 15, the Council of Jerusalem met to discuss evangelizing the world as they knew it. Paul and Barnabas reported what was going on in Gentile regions. They were "men who ... risked their lives for the name of our Lord Jesus Christ" (Acts 15:26, NASB). Missionaries in the Bible experienced their own share of strange encounters.

It is not uncommon in some areas of the world to encounter manifestations of demons. Although a career missionary is used to dealing with such odd occurrences, short-term missionaries can be unprepared to hear demons speak through a possessed person.

Satan does not want you to go into his territory. You might even be shocked, like Renee from Worcester State College was, when encountering his domain. She says:

Our student groups set off each morning to do park ministry and prayerwalking through Sikh, Jain, and Hindu temples in a South Asian city. My crew walked through both the Sikh and the Jain temples without trouble, other than the heavy sadness we felt for the faithful worshipers who had no knowledge of Jesus. When we entered the Hindu temple, we were overwhelmed by the strong sour smell of milk that was poured over idols in adoration. We had to take our shoes off and walk through a milky, sewer-like hallway to the main worship room. The room held a huge, blue idol in a glass case. There were people lying on the floor in front of it, others had their hands raised in worship, and still others were singing aloud to it.

My stomach turned, and I couldn't stop myself from crying. Others in my group were experiencing the same spiritual heaviness. Our hearts were broken for these people and because God Himself watched people worship a blue figure in a box. We all had a tremendous desire for the world to acknowledge God and worship Him.

Jenni from Valdosta State University also faced challenges as a summer missionary.

The typical daily schedule for our team consisted of riding about 25 to 30 miles on a bicycle, setting up camp, prayerwalking through a town, camping out, and conducting surveys.

There were days when we did not know where we would camp, what we would eat, or what we would do if it rained. God never fails us or forsakes us. He was my strength when I was weak. There were days when I thought I could not pedal one more time, when the wind was blowing against us and Satan was trying to keep us out of places. God gave me the strength and perseverance to finish.

Another student, Cortney from Florida State University, discovered that living on the edge with Christ is full of adventure.

One cannot drive a car in which the steering wheel is on the right side and people drive on the left side of the road without facing a few challenges. My teammate and I came to a bridge that was about as wide as the car itself and was missing two or three boards. My partner wanted to turn around. I said that if we floored it, we could just fly over. So we did and when we landed, we bottomed out on something big that left the front right tire about three feet off the ground.

We inspected the damage and did what any normal person stuck in the Asian jungle with no form of communication would do ... we yelled. Of course, it didn't matter what we yelled because as far out as were, not a soul spoke English. I think I tried "Fire!" and "Oh my goodness, I'm not going to see my 20th birthday!" We tried to push the car, to no avail, so we just decided to see what happened.

I sang, played hopscotch, and tried to climb a tree but fell out of it. Finally, a man came by with his truck. He wanted to get through, and we were blocking his path. So he pulled our car out. And while we waited . . . we talked about Jesus.

I wanted to learn the culture, learn the language, and do whatever the people there did. If they decided to have fish heads for breakfast, I was in. I also learned that as a follower of Jesus Christ, my identity does not change. No matter where I am or what I'm doing, my identity is in Christ. And therefore, my heart can't help but be motivated to share that love with whomever I come into contact.

Do you want to be in on the grand adventure? Then take a risk. Accept the challenge. Face the different. Join God on mission.

APPLY IT

1. Read Acts 19:11–20. Although this story is about unbelievers encountering demons, what would you do if you encountered a demon-possessed person on the mission field? Read Matthew 17:14–21. What was Jesus' complete answer to the disciples' question?

2. How do you think you will handle it when you are expected to eat weird foods or use outside restrooms in a foreign country? How can you mentally prepare yourself so that you won't offend someone?

3. On a scale of 1 to 10 (low to high), what do you think is your level of being open to risk?

For further study (optional):
Think about the last time you took a risk for God. How did that experience change you as a person? How do you think God wants you to grow in this area?

PERSECUTION OF BELIEVERS

In 1 Peter 4:13, we are encouraged to share in the sufferings of Christ. However, in the Western world, we have a hard time believing that Christians all over the world are suffering for their faith. Occasionally, a news report will mention that Christian missionaries have been killed. Unless we make a point to research persecution of Christians, we don't think about it too often. But it's real.

A supervisor for a student team visiting Asia was affected by the faith of a Chinese pastor when Johnnie and his students from Liberty University worshiped with an underground church.

None of us will soon forget walking down dark alleys to a home crowded outside with bicycles. Their songs of praise inside seemed to steer us toward the door of this congested, makeshift church. These believers met together with a risky faith. At any moment, the Chinese police could burst through the door. This threat had not silenced them. The potential persecution only seemed to amplify their faith. I guess that was our big lesson of the day—persecution amplifies our faith.

We will not forget meeting a Chinese preacher and attending his illegal house church. How does spending 20 years of your life pointlessly pounding rocks to gravel in a prison camp sound? Twenty years he was absent from his family, church, home ... from everything. Yet he smiled, and not the smile of a half-crazy man. His face was the face of a man who had discovered some great, lost treasure. His words sent shivers up our spines and conviction deep into our souls: "Oh, my dear friends, never forget ... persecution is good."

Do you consider persecution as being good? Most of us probably wouldn't. Persecution usually involves pain. In Matthew 5:10–12, Jesus said, "Blessed are those who have been persecuted for the sake of righteousness, for theirs is the kingdom of heaven. Blessed are you when men cast insults at you, and persecute you, and say all kinds of evil against you falsely, on account of Me. Rejoice and be glad, for your reward in heaven is great, for so they persecuted the prophets who were before you" (NASB). Jesus also said, "If they persecuted Me, they will also persecute you" (John 15:20, NASB).

You probably haven't experienced persecution to the extent that Christians in other countries have. But students you might encounter overseas will understand that being a Christian can bring suffering.

Tyler from Union University met students who will likely face persecution for committing to Christ.

In an atheistic country, students are taught there is no God. However, upon reaching college age, these students learn to ponder life's questions. While at a university in a large Asian city, it was not uncommon for a student to ask, "Will you teach me about God and the Bible?" I didn't expect this. Many students are eager to practice their English with Westerners, but more importantly, they are beginning to question what they've been taught. Conversing with these students was not easy, especially when security officers would be on every street corner watching our every move.

"Many of the students we talked to in Asia said that if they became Christians, they would be kicked out of their families," said Libba from

Mississippi State University. "They needed to think more about it."

Persecution also was encountered by a Canadian student, Christine from McMaster University, in a country in the Pacific Rim.

> We secretly delivered 40 Bibles to two [national] pastors. These pastors are carefully watched by the government but have a passion to spread the good news. ... [Our team] experienced to a small degree what the believers [in this country] face on a regular basis: the lack of freedom to speak the name of Jesus, to pray in public places, and to express God's love in conversation. There was a sense of gratitude for the religious freedom we take for granted in Canada. It was very encouraging to meet with people who are truly willing to risk their lives for the one, true, living God.

Another student, Sara from the University of Mobile, experienced a degree of persecution for her faith in Macedonia. She said,

> There were always people who did not want to hear our message. It would have been easy to become discouraged, but we had to remember it was not **us** that they were rejecting.

Don't forget that as a student missionary, God is the one who has called you to go. And He's big enough to handle rejection.

If you are going to be a student missionary, then you need to count the cost. First, you need to think about the nationals you'll meet with because you put them at risk of being arrested, harmed, or even killed if they live in an anti-Christian country. Security instructions, given by

Christian workers who live overseas, need to be followed completely. You do not want to jeopardize their work in any way. Second, you need to be aware that you could be persecuted while on the mission field.

Christian songwriter and vocalist Rick Heil from Sonicflood encourages other Christians to be "fearless for Jesus" while serving overseas in a country where believers are persecuted.

> When I went to the Muslim nation of Turkey, I met people who had given up everything to follow Jesus. They had been excommunicated from their families, and some had even lost their jobs. Yet the peace and the joy they shared far surpassed the sacrifices they had made to have the freedom that only Jesus Christ can bring. So I challenge you to be fearless for Jesus in this dark world so that generations may be set free!

A verse to keep in your heart is Hebrews 13:6: "The Lord is my helper, I will not be afraid. What shall man do to me?" (NASB). Being a Christian is risky, but as a believer, you are in God's hands.

APPLY IT

1.   Read 2 Timothy 3:12. Why do you think Paul says this?

2.   What should be the reason we are persecuted?
     Read 2 Timothy 2:8–10.

3.   Have you ever been persecuted for your faith? If so, explain.
     If not, how do you feel about the potential of being persecuted?

4.   Read Matthew 5:44. What should you do when persecuted?

For further study (optional):
Read the story of Stephen in Acts 7.

RISKING IT ALL FOR JESUS

Throughout this six-week study, you've discovered that being a Christian involves risk. You take a chance when you pray for the nations, follow God's call to missions, trust Him, get out of your comfort zone and tell others about Christ. It's up to you. You can choose to surrender to Jesus and the life He desires for you, whatever that may be, or you can choose to turn your back on His desires.

The rich young ruler decided the cost was too great to follow Jesus (Matt. 19:16–24). However, a woman mentioned in Matthew 26:6–13 chose to take a risk for Jesus. She was willing to give up two very valuable things: costly perfume (perhaps all her wealth) and her reputation. While Jesus was at someone's house for a meal, the woman came in unannounced and poured expensive perfume on Jesus' head. The disciples thought this act was ridiculous. "Why this waste? This perfume might have been sold for a high price and the money given to the poor," Judas said. But Jesus stood up for the ridiculed woman and said that she had done a good thing.

If you decide to live a godly life, become a living sacrifice, and radically follow Jesus, some people will say to you, "Why this waste? You might have been of better use to society if you had not wasted your life by being a sold-out Christian." If following Jesus involves a student mission trip, some will say, "Why help those people? Don't you know they're terrorists? They hate Christians. You should stay home and get a good-paying summer job."

Jesus tells us, "If anyone wishes to come after me, let him deny himself, and take up his cross, and follow Me" (Matt. 16:24, NASB). Although following Him can mean giving up a variety of things, He asks all Christians to deny themselves and follow Him in whatever He asks.

A student from Mercer University, Leanna, learned the difference between playing it safe and taking risks.

Botswana, Africa, is where I ended up teaching youth about sexual abstinence. In Botswana, over half the population is under 20 years old, and 40 percent of all university students are HIV positive. All of these things were a little scary. Over the next few months, God taught me that life is not about playing it safe, but taking risks in His name. I was 100 percent ready to risk everything for God. I knew I had the prayers of many faithful people and God behind me, so what did I have to fear?

My team found ourselves among foreign people desperate for truth, and trusting God, we gave them truth — the Bible! Many accepted Christ and turned their lives around while seeds were planted in others. The change we saw in people is the very reason we took risks.

As Cortney from Florida pointed out, "Jesus can be dangerous. It's dangerous in Asia where speaking His name to a Muslim can be life threatening. Jesus is good, however, even when He isn't safe."

Sometimes students take the risk of working hard with no visible results. Jeff from the University of Mary Hardin-Baylor said,

When most think of mission work, they think of the story of the seeds. Plant, water, and He will grow. Well, I have learned what is overlooked. The soil has to be ready, and in North Africa, it is not. The soil is laden with stones. I am working alongside the Father and moving some stones. It is hard work, and it takes a lot of obedience, but it has to be done in order to plant seeds. I am enjoying moving stones.

As a result of the risks students have taken, barriers have been moved and the way is continuing to be prepared to reach the lost. These risks have led some students to consider an entirely new direction for their lives. One student, Tomas from Dalton State College, was affected by a mission trip to a Muslim country.

The area of Thailand that we were in was 90 percent Muslim, and I was a little apprehensive. We found that the people were extremely open to us and curious to see what we were doing. We helped start two schools, but our main purpose was to be witnesses for Jesus through our work. People couldn't understand why we would spend time, money, and sweat to help them. We were able to share that God's love was the reason we came, and we were able to exceed our expectations of being able to build relationships with the Thai people. The trip had a profound effect on me and my walk with Jesus Christ. The experience I had is causing me to reevaluate my perspective on life and to begin considering a possible future in missions.

Amy from the University of South Florida had a similar experience.

On a trip to China, I expected to serve God and hopefully make a difference during the short time I was there. However, my trip resulted in a lifelong calling. God touched my heart in an amazing way and ignited a passion and calling to reach the world for Christ. I had previously thought that I was meant to get a job in my hometown after college, but now I know I am called to show Christ's love to all nations. It wasn't until I was placed in this situation, a 21-hour plane ride from home, that I was able to discern God's call for my life. Now I am taking Chinese as my foreign language in hopes of returning after college. I would not trade that life-altering experience for the world.

To conclude this study, let's go back to a question we asked earlier: *Is God calling you to go the ends of the earth?* If yes, then go for it with gusto. If not, then pray that God will send out students who are called to reach the lost of the world. You, as a believer, have a significant role in finishing the task of bringing salvation to all the nations.

God be gracious to us and bless us,
And cause His face to shine upon us.
That Thy way may be known on the earth,
Thy salvation among all nations.

—Psalm 67:1–2, NASB

APPLY IT

1. Read Matthew 19:16–24 and Matthew 26:6–13. Contrast the two people. Which person do you think you are more like? Which one do you want to be like?

2. What do you think the student meant when she said, "Jesus can be dangerous"? How have you found this true in your own life?

3. Do you, at this point, feel called to be a student missionary? If yes, why? If not, in what ways can you still participate in missions?

For further study:
Read Genesis 12:3; Isaiah 66:18–19; John 3:16; and Revelation 5:9. What is God's heart for the nations?

FOR THE LEADER:
GROUP DISCUSSION
QUESTIONS

These discussion questions are designed to cover main points in the chapters and to obtain students' viewpoints on topics. For a complete 6–week study, group leaders may download or request free leader materials that include DVD stories of students, leader notes, discussion questions, additional resource information, and optional activities. Go to www.thetask.org/hismission to order or download *Free Leader's Material: My Life, His Mission Leader's Guide and DVD.*

WEEK 1—IMPACT THE WORLD ON YOUR KNEES

Purpose: To find effective ways to pray for the lost

1. Read Matthew 6:9–13. Discuss what Jesus told His disciples to do. Why is prayer the first step to missions involvement?

2. Ask group members to share the personal prayer they wrote that is patterned after the Lord's Prayer.

3. What did you learn about prayerwalking from the student stories and the lesson?

4. How important is it to be "walking with God" at some level in a spiritual sense before we ever attempt a "prayerwalk"?

5. What role did prayer have in Esther's life when she faced a difficult situation? Discuss how she depended on the prayers and fasting of others.

6. When facing spiritual warfare, what are we to do according to Ephesians 6:10–18?

7. What insights did you gain from the lists of prayer requests for a people group (introduction) and prayer requests for you (day 4)?

8. Which answer to prayer that a student witnessed particularly spoke to you and why? Have you experienced an amazing answer to prayer?

9. Could you adopt a people group to pray for on a regular basis? Discuss the possibilities.

10. How does going on a mission trip play an important part in increasing your prayer support for world missions?

11. Read John 17:11–26. Discuss specific ways that Jesus prayed for His disciples and for future believers. Discuss how Jesus' prayer requests can be prayed for today's missionaries and future converts.

12. Take time to pray for each group member. Pray that the students' walk with the Lord will be strengthened. Pray for other issues related to missions.

WEEK 2—GOD'S CALL: RANDOM OR REAL?

Purpose: To consider how God is calling students to participate in missions through praying, giving, or going.

1. Have you ever felt like God might be calling you to be involved in international missions? Explain.

2. Read Hebrews 11:8. How does obedience factor in to being called by God to do something?

3. Why aren't people responding to the Great Commission found in Matthew 28:19–20? Name five reasons found in day 2 and explain.

4. Read Jonah 1; 2:10; and 3:1–5. How did Jonah's initial disobedience get him into trouble? What happened when he finally obeyed?

5. What is the difference between "willing to go, but planning to stay" and "planning to go, but willing to stay"?

6. What are four ways God confirms His call to missions? Has one or more of these confirmed God's call in your life concerning missions?

7. Read aloud 2 Corinthians 10:5.

8. When Satan causes us to doubt God's calling on our lives, what should we do?

9. Read Jeremiah 1:4–7. What was God's message to Jeremiah about his youthful age?

10. In this lesson, which story from student missionaries really stood out to you? How has this story impacted your outlook on missions?

11. What message do you get from the DVD story? Discuss.

12. Spend time praying that God will reveal His will to each group member concerning future mission involvement.

WEEK 3—THE TRUST FACTOR

Purpose: To confront the group members' level of trust in God

1. Why is it hard for many students to trust God?

2. Who in the Bible had a hard time trusting others or had the right circumstances to doubt others and why?

3. Mention Scripture verses from the lesson that tell the benefits of trusting in God.

4. What does it mean to turn your focus away from yourself and to focus instead on Christ?

5. What did you learn about Abraham's trust in God?

6. How can the attitude "It's up to me to save the world" be detrimental to a mission project experience?

7. What are the three categories of students who usually participate in mission projects? How can categories one and two be a problem in an international setting, for the participant, and for the team? Why is category three best, and how can you be a category three student? (Read Revelation 4:11 and Mark 9:35.)

8. Ask for a volunteer to recite Philippians 4:13.

9. Discuss student stories in the lesson that were particularly meaningful and why.

10. How has God spoken to you this week concerning a possible mission project opportunity or a planned one in the near future?

11. What message did you get from the DVD story? Discuss.

12. Spend time praying for each group member concerning the application of what God is teaching them about trusting Him.

WEEK 4—FLEX OR FREAK OUT?
Purpose: To discover that God doesn't always work on our timetable

1. Discuss several examples from the Bible of situations in which apostle Paul's plans changed. What did you learn about Paul in these situations?

2. Read Philippians 4:11–13. How should Christians respond to unexpected circumstances? Can you think of a personal example in which contentment in a difficult situation helped you experience joy?

3. How do you think being flexible helps on a mission experience? What did you learn about flexibility from the student stories?

4. Read Galatians 5:22–23. Which fruit of the Spirit help us to be more flexible and why?

5. What do you think would be the hardest cultural differences to face when in another country? What was difficult for the student in the DVD story "Street Kids from Kenya"?

6. What were Paul's techniques for cross-cultural experiences? Give examples from Scripture.

7. Discuss 1 Corinthians 9:19. How does this verse apply in an international missions setting?

8. Read Philippians 2:5–8. What does it mean to have the same attitude as Christ?

9. Allow group members to share ways that they can be better servants this week.

10. Which student story in the book made the biggest impact on you about being flexible? Why?

11. How did flexibility play a role in the DVD story "Living for Jesus"?

12. Pray for one another to be content in all circumstances and to exemplify the fruit of the Spirit.

WEEK 5—TELL THE STORY
Purpose: To learn to share the gospel and personal salvation story

1. Is sharing the gospel and your own personal Christian story scary? Why or why not? Discuss.

2. Give some examples of people you know who exemplify Jesus through their lifestyles. How has this impacted you and others?

3. Discuss the response of the woman at the well after hearing the words of Jesus. What was the response of the people she told?

4. Do you think you really grasp that most of the world is lost without Jesus? Does it matter? What do you want to do about it?

5. Briefly discuss the main points of Paul's testimony before King Agrippa in Acts 26. What was King Agrippa's response?

6. Ask the group to break up into partners and have each student share his or her salvation story with the partner.

Limit the students to three minutes each to share.
The partners should time each other.

7. Discuss specific student stories in the lesson that encouraged you to share your faith.

8. Why do students need to be sensitive to the culture and the work the missionary or national has already started when serving overseas? Why is dialogue with the field contact important before you begin your service?

9. Read Luke 8:4–15. Describe the three soils and discuss why a discerning spirit is needed on the mission field.

10. Ask if group members made Scripture memory note cards so that they can memorize the scriptures suggested. Commit as a group to memorize these verses.

11. Read Acts 5:17–42. Why did the apostles not stop talking? How do you feel about suffering for the sake of the gospel?

12. Spend time praying as a group about being a godly witness in lifestyle to others, making the most of opportunities given to share Christ, and memorizing the scriptures assigned in this week's lesson.

WEEK 6—RISKY FAITH

Purpose: To decide if group members are willing to risk everything for Jesus

1. What do you think is the biggest risk you might have to take to be a student missionary?

2. After completing this week's lessons, what do you think about the statement: "The safest place to be is in the center of God's will"? Use examples from Scripture or from the student stories to support your thoughts.

3. Are you willing to be persecuted or even die for the sake of the gospel? What do you fear the most about persecution?

4. What encouragement did you receive from Scripture and the student stories concerning persecution?

5. Name some people in the Bible who risked everything for God. What specifically did they risk?

6. Read Joshua 1:9. How do you think this verse will help you as a student missionary?

7. Think about the last time you took a risk for God. How did that experience change you as a person?

8. Discuss the statement made by the Chinese pastor: "Persecution is good." Why do you think he would say that?

9. Why is it important to follow the advice of the field missionary concerning security matters when you are in a hostile environment as a student missionary?

10. Read 2 Timothy 2:8–10. What should be the cause of persecution for Christians?

11. What is the most significant truth that you learned in this six-week study, and how has this truth affected your life?

12. Spend time praying for God to send out workers to the mission field and to pray that all people groups will have a chance to hear the gospel of Jesus Christ.

NOTES

1. Eileen Fraser Crossman, *Mountain Rain* (Wheaton, IL: Shaw, 1994), 35–36.

2. Wesley L. Duewel, *Touch the World Through Prayer* (Grand Rapids: Asbury, 1986), 16.

3. O. Hallesby, *Prayer* (Minneapolis: Augsburg Fortress, 1994), 70.

4. John Piper, *Let the Nations Be Glad* (Grand Rapids: Baker, 2003), 33, 35.

5. Robertson McQuilkin, *The Great Omission* (Waynesboro, GA: Authentic Media, 2002), 13–14.

6. Henry T. Blackaby and Claude V. King, *Experiencing God: Knowing and Doing His Will* (Nashville: Broadman and Holman, 1998).

7. John Piper, *Let the Nations Be Glad,* 112.